The Standard Encyclopedia of

CARNIVAL GLASS

Revised 2nd Edition

Bill Edwards

COLLECTOR BOOKS

A Division of Schroeder Publishing Co., Inc.

The current values in this book should be used only as a guide. They are not intended to set prices, which vary from one section of the country to another. Auction prices as well as dealer prices vary greatly and are affected by condition as well as demand. Neither the Author nor the Publisher assumes responsibility for any losses that might be incurred as a result of consulting this guide.

Acknowledgments

Without the help of the following people, the nearly 300 new and replacement photos would not have been possible for me to find in such a short time, and I thank all my 'Helpers' from the bottom of my heart: Don and Connie Moore, Don and Marian Doyle, Dean and Joan Fry, John and Lucille Britt, Helen Ovellete, Singleton Bailey, Dee Sponser, Joan Nichols, Ray and Verda Asbury, Fred G. Roque Jr., Carl and Eunice Booker, Lee Markley, Shelli and Clint Arsenault, Eugene R. Grosko, and Marie Martin.

And a very special thanks to the San Diego Carnival Club for all their interest and help in finding the glass to be photographed.

Dedication

To those who have passed on ... Rose and Joe, Marian, Carleton, Bill Carroll and all the rest who were so much a part of our lives. This book is to say how much we miss you.

Author's Note

I have spent a major portion of my life learning about, living with and writing about Carnival glass. Let me say that aside from the pure pleasure of handling so much of this beautiful glass, I've met so many very wonderful people, I feel my life has been enriched beyond measure by the experience.

I hope my many errors will be excused, and my efforts to aid in the Carnival glass hobby by whatever talents the Lord has given me, remembered. This book is the culmination of all I've learned and a good deal of my soul is here.

I only hope it is adequate.

Introduction

For the benefit of the novice, Carnival glass is that pressed and iridized glass manufactured between 1905 and 1930. It was made by various companies in the United States, England, France, Germany, Australia, Sweden and Finland.

The iridization, unlike the costly art glass produced by Tiffany and his competitors, was achieved by a spray process on the surface of the glass before firing, thus producing a very beautiful product at a greatly reduced cost, giving the housewife a quality product well within her budget.

In addition, Carnival glass was the **last** hand-shaped glass mass-produced in America and remains as a beautiful reminder of the glassmaker's skills.

In this volume, we will show the variety of shapes and colors of Carnival glass and will also attempt to define the patterns by manufacturer and for the first time, put the entire field of Carnival glass into one reference book for the collector.

It is my hope that this effort will bring new interest to this truly beautiful glass and stimulate its growth as a collectible; and my only regret is a lack of space to show every known pattern.

The Dugan Story

The Dugan Glass Company of Indiana, Pennsylvania began production on April 14, 1892 calling itself the Indiana Glass Company with Harry White as its president, operating for less than a year before closing. The vacant plant was first leased, then purchased by Harry Northwood in 1895, and for the next two years poured out a stream of Northwood glass until Northwood decided to join the National Glass Combine and moved his main operation to the old Hobbs, Brockunier plant, leasing the Indiana plant to its managers, Thomas E. Dugan and W.G. Minnemeyer who changed the name to the Dugan Glass Company (also called the American Glass Company).

They produced basically the same sorts of glass as Northwood until 1913 when the name was changed again to the Diamond Glass Company with John P. Elkin as president; H. Wallace Thomas, secretary; D. B. Taylor, treasurer; and Ed Rowland, plant manager. During this time, many Northwood moulds were reworked, a trademark with a "D" within a diamond registered and most of the Carnival glass from the company was produced under the supervision of Thomas Dugan.

The plant operated until 1931 when it was destroyed by fire and never rebuilt because of the Depression that gripped the country and the industry.

The Fenton Story

First organized in April 1905, the Fenton Art Glass Company didn't really materialize until the following July. At that time the glass decorating shop was opened in Martins Ferry, Ohio, in an abandoned factory rented by Frank L. Fenton and his brother, John (who was later to found the famous Millersburg Glass Company).

The next few months were occupied in obtaining financial backers, glass workers, buying land to be plotted into lots as a money-raising venture, and construction of their own plant in Williamstown, West Virginia. At times, everything seemed to go wrong, and it wasn't until 1907 that the company was "on its way."

From the first, the design abilities of Frank Fenton were obvious, and each pattern seemed to bear his own special flair. He (along with Jacob Rosenthal who had come to the Fenton factory after fire had destroyed the renowned Indiana Tumbler and Goblet Company in Greentown, Indiana) was greatly responsible for sensing what the vast public admired in glass ornamentation.

In 1908, friction arose between the two brothers, and John exited to pursue his dreams in Millersburg, Ohio. By this time, the Fenton process of iridization had taken the mass-scale art glass field by storm and "Carnival glass" was on its way.

For the next 15 years, the Fenton Company would produce the largest number of patterns ever in this beautiful product, and huge amounts of iridized glass would be sent to the four corners of the world to brighten homes. While the company made other decorative wears in custard, chocolate glass, mosaic inlaid glass, opalescent glass and stretch glass, nothing surpassed the quality and quantity of their iridized glass. Almost 150 patterns are credited to the company in Carnival glass alone, and many more probably credited to others may be of Fenton origin.

All this is truly a remarkable feat, and certainly Frank L. Fenton's genius must stand along side Harry Northwood's as inspiring.

The Imperial Story

While the Imperial Glass Company of Bellaire, Ohio, was first organized in 1901 by a group of area investors, it wasn't until January 13, 1904, that the first glass was made; and not until nearly five years later the beautiful iridized glass we've come to call Carnival glass was produced.

In the years between these dates, the mass market was sought with a steady production of pressed glass water sets, single tumblers, jelly jars, lamp shades and chimneys, and a full assortment of table items such as salt dips, pickle trays, condiment bottles and oil cruets.

All of this was a prelude, of course, to the art glass field which swept the country, and in 1909 Imperial introduced their iridescent line of blown lead lustre articles as well as the Nuruby, Sapphire and Peacock colors of Carnival glass.

As was quite evident then, as now, this proved to be the hallmark of their production. Huge quantities of the iridized glass were designed, manufactured and sold to the mass market-place across America and the European Continent for the next decade in strong competition with the other art glass factories. Especially sought was the market in England early in 1911.

In quality, Imperial must be ranked second only to the fine glass produced by the Millersburg Company and certainly in design, is on an equal with the great Northwood Company. Only the Fenton Company produced more recognized patterns and has outlasted them in longevity (the Imperial Glass Company became a subsidiary of the Lenox Company in 1973).

Along the way came the fabulous art glass line called "Imperial Jewels" in 1916. This was an iridescent product often in free hand worked with a "stretch" effect. This is so popular today, many glass collectors have large collections of this alone.

In 1929, Imperial entered the machine glass era and produced its share of what has come to be called Depression glass and in the early 1960's, the company revived their old molds and reproduced many of the old iridized patterns as well as creating a few new ones for the market that was once again invaded by "Carnival glass Fever." While many collectors purchased these items, purists in Carnival glass collecting have remained loyal to the original and without question, the early years of Carnival glass production at the Imperial Company will always be their golden years.

The Millersburg Story

Interestingly enough, if John and Frank Fenton hadn't had such adverse personalities, there would have been no Millersburg Glass Company. Both brothers had come to the Martins Ferry, Ohio area in 1903 to begin a glass business in partnership, but Frank was conservative and level headed while John was brash and eager - a constant dreamer and the pitch-man of the family. Each wanted to make a name in the business, and each wanted to do it his way.

By 1908, with the Fenton Art Glass Factory going strong, the clashes multiplied, and John went in search of a location for a plant of his own. He was 38, a huge strapping man with a shock of heavy brown hair and a pair of steely eyes that could almost hypnotize. He would sire five children.

After weeks of travel and inquiry, he came to Holmes County, Ohio, and was immediately impressed with the land and the people. Here were the heartland Americans whose families had come from Germany and Switzerland. They were hard workers like the Amish that lived among them, good businessmen who led a simple life.

Word soon spread that John Fenton wanted to build a glass plant, and the people welcomed him. By selling his interest in the Fenton plant and borrowing, John secured option on a 54.7 acre site on the north edge of Millersburg. Lots were plotted and sold, and ground was broken on September 14, 1908. And like John Fenton's dreams, the plant was to be the grandest ever. The main building was 300' x 100', spanned by steel framing with no center supporting. A second building, 50' x 300' was built as a packing and shipping area as well as a tool shop. The main building housed a 14-pot furnace, a mix room, an office area, a lehr area and a display area for samples of their production.

During construction, gas wells were drilled to supply a source of power and stocks were sold in the company, totaling $125,000.00.

On May 20, 1909, the first glass was poured. The initial moulds were designed by John Fenton and were **Ohio Star** and **Hobstar and Feather**. While at the Fenton factory, he had designed others, including the famous "Goddess of Harvest" bowl as a tribute to his wife. The glass that now came from the Millersburg factory was the highest quality of crystal and sample toothpick holders in the **Ohio Star** pattern were given to all visitors that first week.

In addition to the crystal, iridized glass in the Fenton process was put into production the first month in amethyst, green and a soft marigold. A third pattern - a design of cherry clusters and leaves - was added and soon sold well enough to warrant new moulds, bringing the Multi-Fruit and Flowers design into being as a follow-up pattern.

Early in January 1910 the celebrated "Radium" process was born. It featured a softer shade of color and a watery, mirror-like finish on the front side of the glass only; it soon took the glass world by storm and became a brisk seller. Noted glassworker, Oliver Phillips, was the father of the process, and it was soon copied by the Imperial company and others in the area.

In June of that same year, the famous **Courthouse** bowl was produced as a tribute to the town and to the workers who had laid the gas lines to the factory. These bowls were made in lettered, unlettered, radium and satin finish and were given away by the hundreds at the factory, just as the crystal **Ohio Star** punch sets had been given to all the town's churches and social organizations and the famous **People's Vase** was to be made as a tribute to the area's Amish.

During the next year, the Millersburg plant was at its zenith, and dozens of new patterns were added to the line from moulds produced by the Hipkins Mold Company. They included the noted **Peacock** patterns as well as the **Berry Wreath, Country Kitchen, Poppy, Diamond, Pipe Humidor** and **Rosalind** patterns. But by late March 1911, Hipkins wanted pay for their work, as did other creditors, and John Fenton found his finances a disaster. The plant was kept producing, but bankruptcy was filed, and Samuel Fair finally bought the works in October, renaming it the Radium Glass Company. In the next few months, only iridized glass in the radium process was produced while John Fenton tried to find a way to begin again.

But time soon proved Fair couldn't bring the factory back to its former glory, and he closed the doors, selling the factory and its contents to Frank Sinclair and the Jefferson Glass Company in 1913. Sinclair shipped many of the crystal and carnival moulds to the Jefferson plant in Canada for a run of production there which included **Ohio Star, Hobstar and Feather** and Millersburg **Flute**. The rest of the moulds were sold for scrap despite the success of the patterns with the Canadians who bought the graceful crystal designs for several years. Jefferson's production at the Millersburg plant itself was brief. The known pieces include a six inch **Flute** compote just like the famous Millersburg **Wildflower**, marked "Crys-tal" with no interior pattern.

In 1919, the empty plant was again sold to the Forrester Tire and Rubber Company; the great stack was leveled and the furnace gutted. The Millersburg Glass factory was no more. But as long as one single piece of its beautiful glass is collected, its purpose will stand, and the lovers of this beautiful creation will forgive John Fenton his faults in business and praise his creative genius.

The Northwood Story

An entire book could be written about Harry Northwood, using every superlative the mind could summon and still fail to do justice to the man, a genius in his field. Of course, Harry had an advantage in the glass industry since his father, John Northwood, was a renowned English glass maker.

Harry Northwood came to America in 1880 and first worked for Hobbs, Brockunier and Company of Wheeling, West Virginia, an old and established glass producing firm. For five years, Harry remained in Wheeling, learning his craft and dreaming his dreams.

In 1886, he left Hobbs, Brockunier and was employed by the Labelle Glass Company of Bridgeport, Ohio, where he advanced to the position of manager in 1887. A few months later, a devastating fire destroyed much of the LaBelle factory, and it was sold in 1888.

Harry next went to work for the Buckeye Glass Company of Martin's Ferry, Ohio. Here he remained until 1896 when he formed the Northwood Company at Indiana, Pennsylvania. Much of the genius was now being evidenced, and such products as the famous Northwood custard glass date from this period.

In 1899, Northwood entered the National Glass combine only to become unhappy with its financial problems, and in 1901 he broke away to become an independent manufacturer once again. A year later, he bought the long-idle Hobbs, Brockunier plant, and for the next couple of years, there were two Northwood plants.

Finally in 1904, Northwood leased the Indiana, Pennsylvania plant to its managers, Thomas E. Dugan and W. G. Minnemeyer, who changed the name of the plant to the Dugan Glass Company (in 1913 the plant officially became known as the Diamond Glass Company and existed as such until it burned to the ground in 1931).

In 1908, Harry Northwood, following the success of his student Frank L. Fenton in the iridized glass field, marketed his first Northwood iridescent glass, and Northwood Carnival glass was born. For a 10 year period, Carnival glass was the great American "craze" and even at the time of Harry Northwood's death in 1921, small quantitites were still being manufactured. It had proved to be Northwood's most popular glass, the jewel in the crown of a genius, much of it marked with the well-known trade mark.

Other American Companies

Besides the five major producers of Carnival glass in America, several additional companies produced amounts of iridized glass.

These companies include: the Cambridge Glass Company of Cambridge, Ohio; the Jenkins Glass Company of Kokomo, Indiana; the Westmoreland Glass Company of Grapeville, Pennsylvania; the Fostoria Glass Company of Moundsville, West Virginia; the Heisey Glass Company of Newark, Ohio; the McKee-Jeanette Glass Company of Jeanette, Pennsylvania; and the U.S. Glass Company of Pittsburgh, Pennsylvania.

The Cambridge Company was the "leader" of the lesser companies, and the quality of their iridized glass was of a standard equal to that of the Millersburg Glass Company. Actually, there appears to have been a close working relationship between the two concerns, and some evidence exists to lead us to believe some Cambridge patterns were iridized at the Millersburg factory. The Venetian vase is such an item. Known Cambridge patterns are:

Horn of Plenty	Inverted Thistle
Sweetheart	Double Star (Buzz
Buzz Saw Cruet	Saw)
Cologne Bottle	Near Cut Souvenir
Forks Cracker Jar	Proud Puss
Inverted Feather	Tomahawk
Inverted Strawberry	Toy Punch Set
Near-Cut Decanter	Venetian

Many of the Cambridge patterns are beautiful near-cut designs or patterns intaglio; and while amethyst and blue are colors rarely found, most Cambridge Carnival glass was made in green and marigold.

The Jenkins Glass Company made only a handful of Carnival glass patterns, mostly in marigold color, and nearly all patterns in intaglio with a combination of flower and near-cut design. Their known patterns are:

Cane and Daisy Cut	Stork Vase
Cut Flowers	Fleur De Lis Vase
Diamond and Daisy	Oval Star and Fan
Cut	Stippled Strawberry

The Westmoreland Company also made quality Carnival glass in limited amounts. Known patterns are:

Checkerboard	Strutting Peacock
Footed Drape	Pillow and Sunburst
Footed Shell	Shell and Jewel
Basketweave and	Wild Rose Wreath
Cable	#270
Prisms	Corinth Vt.
Orange Peel	Carolina Dogwood
Fruit Salad	

The Fostoria Company had two types of iridized glass. The first was their Taffeta Lustre line which included console sets, bowls and candlesticks; the second was their brocaded patterns which consisted of an acid cutback design, iridized and decorated with gold. These patterns include:

Brocaded Acorns	Brocaded Palms
Brocaded Daffodils	Brocaded Rose
Brocaded Summer	
Garden	

Heisey made very few iridized items and those found have a light, airy luster. Patterns known are:

Covered Frog	Heisey #357
Covered Turtle	Heisey Flute
Heisey Tray Set	Panelled Heisey

The McKee-Jeanette Company had a few Carnival glass patterns as follows:

Aztec	Rock Crystal
Heart Band Souvenir	Sea Gulls Bowl
Lutz	Snow Fancy
Hobnail Panels	

The U.S. Glass Company was a combine of 17 companies, headquartered in Pittsburgh, Pennsylvania. Their plants were usually designated by letters, and it is nearly impossible to say what item came from which factory. However, some of the patterns we have classified as U.S. Glass are:

Beads and Bars	Louisville Shrine
Daisy in Oval Panels	Rochester Shrine
Field Thistle	Champagne
Golden Harvest	Shrine Toothpick
New Orleans Shrine	Palm Beach
Champagne	Vintage Wine
Feather Swirl	Butterfly Tumbler
Cosmos and Cane	

In addition to all the glass produced by these minor concerns, specialty glass houses contributed their share of iridized glass in the large Gone-With-The-Wind lamps, shades, chimneys, etc; as well as minute amounts of iridized glass from Libby, Anchor-Hocking, Tiffin, Devilbiss, Hig-Bee, and Jeanette are known.

It is not possible in our limited space to show all these patterns from the smaller makers, but we'll try to give a sampling from many of them.

In addition, many patterns in Carnival glass have not been attributed to definite producers at this time, and so you will find a few items shown where we must say "maker unknown." While we wish this didn't have to be, sooner or later, these too will find their proper place in the history of Carnival glass.

Non-American Carnival Glass Makers

Besides the British and Australians, factories in Sweden, Finland, Denmark, Czechoslovakia, Holland, Mexico, France and Argentina are now known to have produced some amount of iridized glass. While it would be impossible for us to catalogue all these companies, I will list a few of the more prolific and their currently known patterns.

Finland
Finish Carnival Glass wasn't made until the early 1930's and primarily at four factories, including one at Riihimaki which seemed to specialize in copying some best selling American patterns like Lustre Rose, Four Flowers and Tiger Lily.

Czechoslovakia
Several researchers trace such patterns as Zipper Stitch, The Fish Vase and the Hand Vase to this country's production. If so, they also made some red for I have seen one red Hand vase! Everything else named is in a marigold including the Star and Fan Cordial set.

Sweden
Swedish Carnival glass was in the Varmland region at a factory called the Eda Glassworks with such patterns as Rose Garden, Curved Star, Sunk Daisy and Sunflower and Diamonds. Colors are primarily marigold and blue, and I suspect the Sungold Epergne may have come from this factory.

Argentina
The Regolleau Cristalerias Company is in Buenos Aires, and here a handful of little-known patterns were made including the Beetle Ash Tray, and an ash tray I call CR since that is just how it is shaped. I've seen it in both marigold and blue.

Mexico
Recent information into the mysterious patterns of Voltive Light, Ranger and Oklahoma all point to a Mexican production by Cristales de Mexico in Nuevo Leon, Mexico. Each of these patterns is marked with the "M" inside a "C."

In addition, small amounts of iridized glass, often decorated with hand painting, was made in France, Germany, Holland and Belgium. Some of these pieces are very intricate and the design top-notch. I have seen a very beautiful custard glass bowl in a bride's basket that has a candy-ribbon edge; it is iridized and has an enamel design. It was pretty enough to be in a museum, and I've envied the owner ever since I saw it.

English Carnival Glass

When iridized glass caught the buyer's fancy in this country, the major companies (especially Imperial and Fenton) began to ship Carnival glass to England, Europe and Australia, and it wasn't long until the glass houses there began to enter the iridized field. In England, the chief producer of this glass was the Sowerly Company of Gateshead-on-Tyne. However, other concerns made some iridized glass, including Gueggenheim, Ltd., of London; and Davisons of Gateshead.

The movement of Carnival glass in England began later than in America and lasted about five years after sales had diminished in this country. Many shapes were made, including bowls, vases, compotes and table pieces. However, water sets and punch sets were pretty much overlooked, and only a few examples of these have come to light. Colors in English glass were mainly confined to marigold, blue and amethyst, but an occasional item in green does appear. The pastels apparently were not popular for few examples exist.

Here then is a list of known English patterns and its volume may surprise many collectors:

African Shield	Hobstar Reversed
Apple Panels	Illinois Daisy
Art Deco	Intaglio Daisy
Banded Grape and	Kokomo
Leaf	Lattice Heart
Beaded Hearts	Lea (and variants)
Buddha	May Basket
Cane and Scroll	Moonprint
Cathedral Arches	My Lady's
(Hobstar and	Powderbox
Cathedral	Pineapple
Chariot	Pinwheel
Covered Hen	Pinwheel Vase
Covered Swan	Sacic Ashtray
Daisy Block	Saint Candlestick
Daisy and Cane	Signet
Diamond Ovals	Spiralex
Diving Dolphins	Split Diamond
Fans	Star
Feathered Arrow	Stippled Diamond
Fine Cut Rings	Swag
Flute Sherbet	Thistle and Thorn
Footed Prism Panels	Tiny Berry Tumbler
Grape and Cherry	Triads
Heavy Prisms	Vining Leaf
Hobstar Cut Triangles	Scroll Embossed Vt.

Australian Carnival Glass

Just as England caught the "fever," so did the populace of Australia and in 1918, the Crystal Glass Works, Ltd., of Sydney began to produce a beautiful line of iridized glass, whose finish ranks with the very best; mostly in bowls and compotes, but with occasional table items and two water sets known.

Australian Carnival glass is confined to purple, marigold, and an unusual amber over aqua finish and patterns known are:

Australian Swan	Kiwi
Banded Diamonds	Kookaburra (and
Butterflies and Bells	variants)
Butterflies and	Pin-Ups
Waratah	Emu (Ostrich)
Butterfly Bower	Rose Panels
Butterfly Bush	S-Band
Flannel Flower	Sun Gold Epergne
Flannel Berry	Thunderbird (Shrike)
Kangaroo (and	Waterlily and
variants)	Dragonfly
Kingfisher (and	Wild Fern
variant)	Golden Cupid
Magpie	Feathered Flowers
Crystal Cut	Blocks and Arches
Australian Grape	Interior Rays
Beaded Spears	

ABSENTEE DRAGON

If you will take a close look at this very rare 9″ plate, you will see it is very different from the Dragon and Berry pattern it resembles. It is the only one known and while I hate the name, I consider it a top rarity in Fenton glass. It has a Bearded Berry reverse pattern, and the color is excellent. It was, no doubt, an experimental piece.

ACANTHUS

Found both in many shaped bowls and plates, the Acanthus was once considered to be a Millersburg pattern, but old Imperial catalogs have proved its origin as Imperial. The colors are usually marigold or smoke, but I show the pattern in green, and I'm sure amethyst is a strong possibility. The mold work is good, and the glass quality and the iridescence very good.

ACORN (FENTON)

It would be hard to imagine a more naturalistic pattern than this. Realistic acorns and oak leaves arranged in three groupings, filling much of the allowed space, form a very pleasing design. Acorn is found on both bowls and plates in a wide range of colors including marigold, amethyst, green, red, vaseline, ice blue and iridized milk glass.

ACORN (MILLERSBURG)

Rarely found, this beautiful compote is typically Millersburg in several respects. First, the shape of the stem and the clover-leaf type base are found on several compotes of the Ohio company. Add to that the fine detail of the design, the excellent workmanship, and if that isn't enough, the typical Millersburg colors of green or amethyst, and that should convince anyone. A rare vaseline is known, but a marigold acorn compote would be a real find.

ACORN BURRS

Other than the famous Northwood Grape and their Peacock at Fountain pattern, Acorn Burrs is probably the most respresentative of the factory's work, and one eagerly sought by Carnival glass collectors. The pattern background is that of finely done oak bark while the leaves are those of the chestnut oak. The moldwork is well done and the coloring ranks with the best. Acorn Burrs is found in a wide range of colors and shapes and always brings top dollar.

ADVERTISING ITEMS

These come in dozens of varieties, several shapes and colors, and it would be impossible in our limited space to show them all. Advertising items were a much welcomed area of business by **all** carnival glass makers because they were a guaranteed source of income without the usual cost-lost factor of unsold stock. Also, they could often be made with less care since they were to be given away; old molds could often be utilized, avoiding expensive new molds. Many Northwood advertising items were small plates with simple floral designs.

AFRICAN SHIELD

This small vase-shape originally had a wire flower holder that held the stems of freshly cut blossoms in a neat arrangement. It is 2⅞″ tall and 3¼″ wide at the top, and while I can't be certain who made it, I believe it is English. Marigold is the only color reported so far.

Absentee Dragon

Acanthus

Acorn (Fenton)

Acorn (Millersburg)

Acorn Burrs

Advertising Items

African Shield

AGE HERALD

Once thought to be a Millersburg item, we are now convinced the Age Herald bowls and plates were made by Fenton. Found only in amethyst, the Age Herald was a give-away item from the Birmingham, Alabama newspaper. It has an exterior pattern of wide panels and is a scarce and expensive pattern.

AMARYLLIS

This unusual compote is a treasure for several reasons. First is the size (2¼″ tall, 5¼″ wide). The shape is roughly triangular, rising from a slightly domed base. The underside carries the Poppy Wreath pattern, and the only colors reported are a deep purple, cobalt blue and marigold.

Amaryllis is a rather scarce Northwood pattern and isn't often mentioned in carnival glass discussions. It is, however, a unique and interesting addition to any collection.

APPLE AND PEAR INTAGLIO

Like its cousin, the Strawberry Intaglio, this rather rare bowl is a product of the Northwood Company and is seen mostly in crystal or goofus glass. The example shown measures 9¾″ in diameter and is 2¾″ tall. The glass is ½″ thick!

APPLE BLOSSOM TWIGS

This is a very popular pattern, especially in plates where the design is shown to full advantage. The detail is quite nice with fine mold work, much like that of Acorn Burrs. Found mostly in marigold, peach and purple, Apple Blossom Twigs has as its exterior pattern, the Big Basketweave pattern. Shards in this pattern at the Dugan site have been identified.

APPLE BLOSSOMS

Found only in small bowls or plates, Apple Blossoms seems to be an average Carnival glass pattern, produced for a mass market in large quantities. Most often seen in marigold, it is occasionally found in vivid colors as well as pastels, especially white. A quarter size chunk of this pattern in white was found at the Dugan dump site in 1975.

APPLE PANELS

There is some dispute about the origin of this cute breakfast set; some say Imperial, others England. I personally feel Apple Panels is a British pattern because so many examples come from there. However, the pattern is known in green which is unusual for English glass.

The pattern is all intaglio and no other shapes are known. Green and marigold are the only reported colors.

Age Herald

Amaryllis

Apple and Pear Intaglio

Apple Blossom Twigs

Apple Blossoms

Apple Panels

APPLE TREE

It certainly is a pity Fenton chose to use this realistic pattern on water sets only. It would have made a beautiful table set or punch set. Apple Tree is available in marigold, cobalt blue and white, and I've seen a rare vase whimsey formed from the pitcher with the handle omitted. The coloring is nearly always strong and bright.

APRIL SHOWERS

Like the bubbles in a carbonated soft drink, the tiny beads seem to float over this very interesting vase pattern. Found in all sizes from 5″ to 14″, April Showers is sometimes found with Peacock Tail pattern on the interior. The colors are marigold, blue, purple, green and white. The top edge is usually quite ruffled in the Fenton manner.

ARCS

This pattern is often confused by beginning collectors with the Scroll Embossed pattern, and it's easy to see why. Perhaps they were designed by the same person since they are both Imperial patterns. Arcs is found on bowls of average size, often with an exterior of File pattern and on compotes with a geometric exterior. The usual colors are marigold or a brilliant amethyst, but green does exist as does smoke.

ART DECO

We don't often see such a plain Carnival pattern, but this one has a good deal of interest, despite its lack of design. The very modern look was all the rage in the art deco age so I've named this cute little bowl in that manner. I don't know who the English manufacturer was.

AURORA PEARLS

Here is a piece of beauty no matter if you're a Carnival glass lover or not. It is European, I think, on custard glass, iridized and decorated. If I ever see one for sale, it will be mine for I really am taken by this bowl and only wish it were a compote!

AUSTRALIAN FLOWER SET

Used like the Water Lily and Dragonfly flower set, this Australian beauty has no design except the slender thread border on the bowl's exterior. The iridescence is fantastic, as you can see.

AUSTRALIAN GRAPE

I can't confirm the existence of a pitcher to match this tumbler, but I'd guess there is. The marigold color is weak, but the mold work is nice. It is from Australia where it is called Vineyard Harvest.

Aurora Pearls

Apple Tree

April Showers

Arcs

Art Deco

Australian Flower Set

Australian Grape

AUSTRALIAN SUGARS

These two beauties are kissing cousins and both Australian. The marigold one is called Australian Panels and the purple one Australian Diamonds (not Concave Diamonds as previously listed). Other shapes may exist, but I haven't seen them.

AUSTRALIAN SWAN

Pictured is the Australian Black Swan on a very beautiful bowl design. The floral sprays remind us of Lily-of-the-Valley but are probably some Australian plant. Colors are purple and marigold in both large and small bowls.

AUTUMN ACORNS

Apparently a spin-off pattern from the Fenton Acorn, Autumn Acorns has replaced the realistic oak leaf with the grape leaf used on the Vintage pattern bowls. Found mostly in bowls, an occasional plate is seen in green. The bowls are found in marigold, blue, green, amethyst, vaseline and red.

AZTEC

While McKee didn't make much Carnival glass, the few existing pieces are treasures and certainly the Aztec pattern is one. Known only in a creamer, sugar, rosebowl, tumblers and pitcher, the coloring ranges from a good strong marigold to a beautiful clambroth with a fiery pink and blue highlights. Each shape in Aztec is rare and important.

BALLOONS

Balloons is one of those borderline items that could be called either Carnival glass or stretch glass since it has characteristics of both. Found in various shapes, including vases of different sizes and shapes, plates with a center handle, compotes and perfume atomizers. The colors are marigold or smoke. The design is ground through the lustre and appears clear; and, of course, there is the stretch effect on many of the pieces.

BAND OF ROSES

Besides this tumble-up and matching tray, a pitcher and tumbler are known in this pattern. It came from Argentina I understand, but is probably a product of a glass firm in Europe. At any rate, it is pretty and quite rare in any shape.

BANDED DIAMOND

Now known to be an Australian pattern, Banded Diamond is found in water sets and berry sets that are scarce. The colors are a very rich amethyst and a strong marigold.

BANDED DRAPE

Banded Drape is another of Fenton's decorated water sets, but the shape is quite distinctive, being almost urn shaped. The colors are very beautiful with much luster and are found in marigold, amethyst, cobalt blue, white and ice green. The enamelled flower seems to be a lovely calla lilly.

Aztec   **Band of Roses**

Australian Sugars

Australian Swan

Autumn Acorns

Balloons

Banded Diamond

Banded Drape

BANDED GRAPE AND LEAF

Here is the **only** water set I've heard about in English glass. As you can see, the design is quite good, and the color is better than average. The only color I've seen is marigold, and at least two sets of this pattern are in American collections.

BANDED RIB

Probably another rather late pattern, this is one of the taller water sets, probably intended for iced tea or lemonade. The only color reported is the marigold, and the only shapes are tumblers and pitchers.

BASKET

Novelty items are a very important area of glass production, and this little item is one of the best known. Standing on four sturdy feet, the Northwood Basket is about 5¾″ tall and 5″ across. Often the basket is simply round, but sometimes one finds an example that has been pulled into a six-sided shape. Made in a wide range of colors including marigold, purple, vaseline, cobalt, ice green, ice blue, aqua and white. This is a popular pattern.

BASKETWEAVE (NORTHWOOD)

Here's a secondary Northwood pattern found often on bowls and now and then on compotes and bon-bons. It's a pretty, all-over filler that does the job.

BASKETWEAVE, BIG

This Dugan pattern is found on the exterior of Fanciful and Round-Up bowls, the base pattern for the Persian Garden two-piece fruit bowls and for vases as shown, as well as a miniature handled basket. Colors are marigold, amethyst, blue, peach opalescent and white.

BASKETWEAVE AND CABLE

Much like the Shell and Jewel breakfast set from the same company, the Westmoreland Basketweave and Cable is a seldom found pattern and surely must have been made in limited amounts. The mold work is excellent and the luster satisfactory. Colors are marigold (often pale), amethyst, green and rarely white.

BEADED ACANTHUS

It's hard to believe this outstanding pattern was made in this one shape only, but to date I've heard of no other. This milk pitcher, like the Poinsettia, measures 7″ tall and has a base diameter of 3¾″. It is found mostly on marigold glass or smoke but a very outstanding green obviously exists, and I suspect amethyst is also a possibility. The coloring is usually quite good, and the iridescence is what one might expect from the Imperial Company.

BEADED BAND AND OCTAGON LAMP

Here is a seldom-seen oil lamp that is really very attractive. The coloring is adequate but watery, indicating 1920's production. It was reportedly made in two sizes, 7½″ and 9¾″, but I can't confirm this. The maker is unknown.

Banded Rib

Basketweave (Northwood)

Basket

Banded Grape and Leaf

Basketweave and Cable

Big Basketweave

**Beaded Band and
Octagon Lamp**

Beaded Acanthus

BEADED BASKET

While the Beaded Basket is quite plentiful, especially in marigold, its origin has always been a little in doubt, and I'm placing it here as a Dugan pattern. Actually, the design qualities are quite good and the mold work superior, so any company could well be proud of these cuties. The colors are marigold, purple, blue and smoke, with the blue most difficult to find. Green may exist, but I haven't heard of one, nor have I had any other pastels reported, except the rare vaseline shown.

BEADED BULLS EYE

There are several variations of this vase pattern often caused by the "pulling" or "slinging" to obtain height. Nevertheless, the obvious rows of bull-eyes on the upper edge serve to establish identity. Found mostly in marigold, these Imperial vases are not easily found.

BEADED CABLE

The Beaded Cable rosebowl has long been a favorite with collectors for it is a simple yet strong design, made with all the famous Northwood quality. Usually about 4″ tall, these rosebowls stand on three sturdy legs. The prominent cable intertwines around the middle and is, of course, edged by beads. Nearly all pieces are marked and are made in a wide variety of colors. Of course, these pieces are sometimes opened out to become a candy dish, like many Northwood footed items.

BEADED PANELS COMPOTE

This little cutie was made by the Westmoreland company and can be found in marigold, amethyst, a rare milkglass with a vaseline finish and the peach opal finish shown. It isn't rare but certainly is a pretty addition to any collection.

BEADED SHELL

Known also in custard glass, Beaded Shell is one of the older Dugan patterns and is found in a variety of shapes, including berry sets, table sets, water sets and mugs. Colors are purple, blue, green, marigold and white with blue and purple somewhat more easily found.

BEADED SPEARS

This previously unlisted Australian water set is a very scarce and beautiful pattern. Besides the peaks of stylized prisms, there are sections of fine file work with unusual circles of plain glass. Other colors and shapes aren't known to me, but certainly may exist.

Beaded Basket

Beaded Bulls Eye

Beaded Cable

Beaded Panels Compote

Beaded Shell

Beaded Spears

BEADED STAR

Most often found on a smallish bowl shape shown, this is a pattern that doesn't receive many raves, nor does it especially deserve them. It is found on rosebowls and a plate shape also in marigold and amethyst.

BEADED SWIRL

This Scandanavian pattern can be found in a covered butterdish, sugar, milk pitcher as well as the compote shown. Colors are marigold and blue, much like the Grand Thistle waterset that was made in Finland and this pattern may well be from the same concern.

BEADS

It's really a shame this pattern isn't found more often and is restricted to the exterior of average size bowls because it is a well-balanced, attractive item, especially on vivid colors. Combining three motifs - daisy-like flowers, petalish blooms and beads - this pattern, while not rare, is certainly not plentiful and is a desirable Northwood item.

BEAUTY BUD VASE (TWIGS)

The most distinctive feature of this vase is, of course, the twig-like feet, intended to be tree roots. These vases are found in sizes from 3½" to 11" tall.

Marigold is the most plentiful color and often only the top shows any hues at all, but the tiny purple version is a beauty and is much sought by vase collectors. Dugan Glass.

BEE ORNAMENT

Like the famous Butterfly Ornaments, the tiny bee is a real rarity and cute as can be (no pun intended). This is the only one I've heard about, but there certainly may be others and even other colors. If so, no one has told me.

BEETLE ASH TRAY

Unusual is the word for this rare ash tray. It was made by the Regolleau Christalerias Company of Buenos Aires, Argentina around 1925. As you can see, the mold work is outstanding, and the cobalt blue coloring is excellent. To date, only two of these have been reported.

BELLAIRE SOUVENIRS

This curious bowl measures 7" in diameter and is roughly 2½" deep. The lettering and little bell are all interior work while the fine ribbing is on the outside. Just when this bowl was given, or why it remains is a mystery to me, but I'm quite sure it would have great appeal to the collector of lettered glass. This was made by Imperial.

BELLS AND BEADS

Shards of this pattern turned up in the Helman digs so we know this is another Dugan pattern. Found in small bowls, plates, hat shapes, nappies, compotes and a handled gravy boat, Bells and Beads' colors are marigold, blue amethyst, green and peach opalescent.

BERNHEIMER BOWL

The only difference between this much sought bowl and the famous Millersburg Many Stars pattern is, of course, the advertising center, consisting of a small star and the words: Bernheimer Brothers. This replaces the usual large star and demonstrates how a clever mold designer can capitalize on a good design. While not nearly as plentiful as the Many Stars bowls, the Bernheimer bowls are found in blue only.

Beetle Ash Tray

Bee Ornament

Beaded Swirl

Beauty Bud Vase (Twigs)

Beads

Beaded Star

Bellaire Souvenirs

Bells and Beads

Bernheimer Bowl

BIG FISH

If there is a single bowl pattern on which the Millersburg reputation could rest, this wouldn't be a bad choice. Like the Millersburg Peacock, the mold work is outstanding, and the realistic portrayal of the species is exceptional. Each scale, each flower petal is so realistically done that the fish almost seems ready to leap from the glass. Here again, a wide variety of bowl shapes were produced, and it is not unusual to see round, square or three cornered ones. Often, the amethyst is a little pale, but the green is marvelous and my personal favorite. Again, we find a wide panel exterior with a rayed base.

BIG THISTLE PUNCH BOWL

I could spend pages raving about this very superb Millersburg rarity, but let me simply say I consider it the most beautiful of all the carnival glass punch bowls. Two are known, and both are amethyst. One has a flared top while the other is straight up. Needless to say, the glass is clear, the mold work superior and the iridescence beyond belief.

BIRD WITH GRAPES

This unusual wall vase is somewhat similar to the woodpecker vase in concept, and I'd guess it too is a product of the Dugan factory, but I can't be positive. The coloring is a pale marigold with an amber tint.

BIRDS AND CHERRIES

Found quite often on bon bons and compotes, this realistic Fenton pattern is sometimes found on rare berry sets and very rare 10" plates. The birds, five in number, remind me of grackles. I've heard of this pattern in marigold, blue, green, amethyst, white, pastel-marigold and vaseline.

BLACKBERRY (FENTON)

Found often as an interior pattern on the open edge basketweave hat shape Fenton produced in great numbers, Blackberry is a very realistic pattern, gracefully molded around the walls of the hat. It is known in many colors including marigold, cobalt blue, green, amethyst, ice blue, ice green, vaseline and red. The example shown is blue with marigold open edge.

BLACKBERRY (FENTON)

This rare Fenton whimsey is shaped from the two-row open edge basket with Blackberry pattern interior. The vase has been shaped into a 8¼" tall beauty. The only color reported is a beautiful cobalt blue but others may certainly exist.

Big Fish

Big Thistle Punch Bowl

Bird With Grapes

Birds and Cherries

Blackberry

Blackberry Whimsey Vase

BLACKBERRY (NORTHWOOD)

While several companies had a try at a Blackberry pattern, Northwood's is one of the better ones and quite distinctive. The pattern covers most of the allowed space, be it the interior of a 6″ compote or an 8½″ footed bowl. Combined with the latter is often a pattern called Daisy and Plume. The colors are marigold, purple, green and white.

BLACKBERRY BANDED

Like many Fenton patterns, Blackberry Banded is limited to the hat shape, and without an exterior pattern. These ruffled hats are usually between 3¼″ and 3¾″ tall, with a base diameter of 2½″. Found mostly in marigold or cobalt blue, they are rarely found in green and rare milk glass with marigold iridization.

BLACKBERRY BLOCK

Make no mistake about it - this is a much underrated water set! Just why it hasn't become more treasured by collectors puzzles me, because it is well made, pretty and quite scarce. Found in marigold, green and cobalt blue, I suspect white was made too, but haven't verified a set in this color yet. Manufactured by Fenton.

BLACKBERRY BRAMBLE

A very available pattern on bowls and compotes, Blackberry Bramble is a very close cousin to the Fenton Blackberry pattern but has more leaves, berries and thorny branches. The bowls are rather small with diameters of 6″ to 8¼″ and the compotes are of average size. Colors are marigold, green and cobalt blue, but others may certainly exist.

BLACKBERRY SPRAY

I've always felt this a poorly designed pattern, but others may disagree. There isn't too much graceful about the four separate branches, and the fruit isn't spectacular. Nevertheless, it can be found on hat shapes, bon bons and compotes, in marigold, cobalt blue, green, amethyst, aqua and red. The aqua does not have opalescence, at least the examples I've seen.

BLACKBERRY WREATH

Apparently one of the early Millersburg patterns Blackberry Wreath is found more often than not without the radium finish. Oddly enough, the basic pattern is like the Millersburg Strawberry except for the center berry and leaf; however, the moldwork is not as distinct, and the glass doesn't have the clarity of the Strawberry pattern. Nevertheless, Blackberry Wreath is a nicely proportioned pattern, especially on the larger bowls. The exterior is usually decorated with a wide panel design and has a many-rayed star on the base, exactly like the Millersburg Peacock and Urn variant.

Blackberry

Blackberry Banded

Blackberry Block

Blackberry Bramble

Blackberry Spray

Blackberry Wreath

BLACK BOTTOM (FENTON)

This very Art Deco little candy jar once had a lid but it has long since been separated. These are shown in the old Fenton ads in a host of colors in stretch glass, but this is the first one I've seen in marigold. The base has a spray-painted finish that has been then fired to keep its black color.

BLOCKS AND ARCHES

Often confused with the very similar Ranger pattern, Blocks and Arches is really an Australian design found only on pitchers and tumblers like the one shown. Colors are marigold and amethyst.

Blocks and Arches

BLOSSOMS AND BAND

Blossoms and Band is not a very distinguished pattern, and its origin is questionable. Found primarily on berry sets in marigold, a car vase is also known, as shown. The design is quite simple with a row of blossoms, stems and leaves above a band of thumbprints and prisms. The color has a good deal of pink in the marigold, much like English glass. The mold work is adequate but far from outstanding. Needless to say, this is not the same pattern as that found on the Millersburg Wild Rose lamps that are often called by the same name. This is possibly an Imperial pattern.

BLOSSOMTIME

Even if this outstanding compote were not marked, we'd surely assign it to the Northwood company because it is so typical of their work. The flowers, the thorny branches (twisted into a geometrical overlapping star) and the curling little branchlets are all nicely done and are stippled, except for the branchlets. The background is plain and contrasts nicely. Blossomtime is combined with an exterior pattern called Wild Flower and is found in marigold, purple, green and pastels. The stem is quite unusual, being twisted with a screw-like pattern. Blossomtime is a scarce pattern and always brings top dollar.

BLUEBERRY

May I say in the beginning, I'm quite prejudiced about this Fenton water set for I think it is outstanding in both design and execution. What a shame it wasn't made in other shapes such as a table set. I've heard of Blueberry in marigold, cobalt blue and white only but that doesn't mean it wasn't made in other colors.

BOOKER MUG

This cutie is in the collection of Carl and Eunice Booker so I've named it after them. It is smaller than most, has a beautiful spray of enamelled flowers and an amethyst handle! It is probably European.

BO PEEP MUG AND PLATE

While the Bo Peep mug is simply scarce, the plate is a quite rare item, seldom sold or traded from one collection to another. The color is good marigold and reminds us of that found on most of the Fenton Kitten items. Of course, all children's items in glass were subjected to great loss through breakage, but I doubt if large amounts of the Bo Peep pattern were made to begin with; so of course small quantities have survived.

BOGGY BAYOU
(PANELLED DIAMOND AND BOWS)

This interesting Fenton pattern is called Panelled and Diamond Bows by Mrs. Presznick, but William Heacock identifies it as Boggy Bayou so I listed both names here. As you can see, it has a roughly geometric panel of diamonds with propeller-like fillers between. These are listed in sizes from 7″ to 11″. The colors I've heard about are marigold, green, blue, amethyst, and white, but probably there are others.

BORDER PLANTS

Again, here is a pattern long regarded as a Fenton product, but it is actually from the Dugan factory. The colors I've seen are amethyst and peach opalescent, but others may exist. The bowl can be found either flat or footed.

Black Bottom (Fenton)

Blossom Time

Blossoms and Band

Blueberry

Bo Peep Mug and Plate

Booker Mug

Boggy Bayou (Panelled Diamond and Bows)

Border Plants

29

BOUQUET

If you look quite closely at this bulbous water set, you'll notice several common devices used by the Fenton Company, such as fillers of scales surrounding an embroidery ring. No other shapes exist, and the water set is found in marigold, blue and white. The mold work is quite good, and the colors are typically Fenton.

BOUTONNIERE

This little beauty is a Millersburg product. It usually has a fine radium finish and is most often seen in amethyst. And although I haven't seen one, I've been told there is a variation sometimes found with a different stem and base. Boutonniere is also found in marigold and green.

HEISEY BREAKFAST SET

While it isn't so marked, I'd guess this very attractive marigold breakfast set was a Heisey product. The coloring is very dark and rich and the handles are like those on known Heisey products.

BROCADED ACORNS

The lacy effects of all these brocaded patterns by the Fostoria company are a joy to behold. This was achieved by an acid-cutback process, and after the iridescence was fired a gold edging was applied. Found in several shapes, Brocaded Acorns was made in pink, white, ice green, ice blue and vaseline.

BROCADED DAFFODILS

Like the other brocaded patterns, this was made by Fostoria. The shape is a 7½" x 6½" handled bowl in pink. The lovely pattern consists of beautifully realistic daffodils, leaf swirls, and small star fillers.

BROCADED PALMS

Shown is one example of Fostoria's Brocaded series, a large handled cake plate in Brocaded Palms pattern. As you can see, the design is created with an acid cutback effect on the glass before iridization, and the edges are gold trimmed. All the patterns are generally handled in this manner and colors found include ice green, ice blue, pink, white and a lovely and rare rose shade, as well as a rare vaseline color.

Bouquet

Boutonniere

Heisey Breakfast Set

Brocaded Acorns

Brocaded Daffodils

Brocaded Palms

BROKEN ARCHES

Broken Arches is a beautiful geometric Imperial pattern found only in punch sets of rather stately size. Not only is the coloring good, but the mold work is outstanding. The colors are marigold and amethyst. Often there is a silver sheen to the latter which detracts from its beauty, but when a set is found without this gun-metal look, the result is breathtaking. The marigold set is more common and sells for much less than amethyst. A green Broken Arches would be a great rarity.

BROOKLYN BOTTLE

I suspect this beautiful 9⅝″ cruet may be of European origin. The glass is very thin, and the non-iridized handle and stopper are very attractive amethyst glass.

BROOKLYN BRIDGE

Like the Pony bowl pattern, this beautiful advertising bowl apparently came from the Dugan factory. The only color reported is marigold, and the mold work is outstanding. Brooklyn Bridge is a scarce and desirable pattern. A rare unlettered example is also known.

BULLS EYE AND LEAVES

Confined to the exterior of bowls and found mostly in green or marigold, this pattern is a trifle too busy to be very effective and is certainly not one of Northwood's better efforts. All in all, there are five motifs, including leaves, beads, circles, fishnet, and a petal grouping. Although each appears on other Northwood products, not in this combination.

BULLS EYE AND LOOP

This Millersburg pattern is much like its sister design, Tulip Scroll, in size and shape, the example shown being 8½″ tall and having a rim diameter of 4″. There are four rows of loops with the bull's eye appearing on alternating loops in a staggered manner. The glass is very clear and the radium finish outstanding. Amethyst is the only reported color but others probably exist. Bull's Eye and Loop is a rather rare pattern, and only four examples have been reported to date.

BUTTERFLIES

This outstanding Fenton pattern is found only on bon-bons often flattened into a card tray shape. The colors are very good with eight butterflies around the edges and one in the center. The exterior carries a typical wide panel pattern and often is found with advertising on the base. Colors are marigold, cobalt blue, green amethyst and white. At least these are the ones I've heard about.

BUTTERFLIES AND WARATAH

Normally seen in the compote shape, this one has been flattened into a very stylish footed cake stand. The beautiful purple is typical of Australian Carnival glass and can stand with the best. It is also found in marigold.

Bull's Eye And Loop

Broken Arches

Brooklyn Bottle

Brooklyn Bridge

Bulls Eye and Leaves

Butterflies

Butterflies and Waratah

BUTTERFLY

The only shape chosen for this Northwood pattern is the bon-bon, and most of the ones I've seen are on amethyst base glass, although marigold and green are found occasionally and pastels have been reported. The pattern shows a lone butterfly in the center of a stippled rays pattern. Not too imaginative but the butterfly shows quite good detail. A variant is known with a ribbed exterior.

BUTTERFLY BOWER

The interior design of a stippled central butterfly flanked by trellis work and flora is hard to see. However, the exterior's S-Band pattern shows quite well. This deep bowl is 6½" across and stands 3" tall. It can be found in marigold and purple. The rim has a bullet edge. Manufactured in Australia.

BUTTERFLY TUMBLER

Shown is one of the most expensive glass tumblers known. This particular example brought more than $4,000.00 in trade and cash a while back, which only proves scarcity plus desire equals big bucks. The Butterfly tumbler is on a pale amberish marigold. The edging design is much like Shell and Jewel, but Butterfly is a U.S. Glass product. A matching footed pitcher has been rumored by not confirmed.

BUTTERFLY AND BERRY

This is certainly one of the Fenton Company's prime designs and can be found on a large array of shapes, including footed berry sets, table sets, water sets, a footed hatpin holder, vases, a rare spittoon whimsey and a rare footed bowl whimsey. Colors are marigold, cobalt blue, green, amethyst, white and rarely red.

BUTTERFLY AND CORN VASE

This interesting vase is rare for several reasons, and it is a pleasure to show it here. First is the pattern which has been reported only twice in the past few years. Both examples are identical in size (5⅞" tall and 2¾" base diameter). Secondly, the base color of the glass is vaseline with a marigold finish. While this coloring is found rarely on both Millersburg and Northwood items, I believe the Butterfly and Corn vase to be a product of the latter.

BUTTERFLY AND FERN

For many years, collectors considered this very beautiful water set a Millersburg product and indeed the color and finish rival products of the Ohio Company, but Butterfly and Fern is a Fenton item for sure. The mold work is outstanding and the available colors of marigold, amethyst, green and blue are marvelous!

BUTTERFLY AND TULIP

Make no mistake about it, this is a very impressive Dugan pattern. The bowl is large, the glass heavy and the mold work exceptional. Found in either marigold or purple, this footed jewel has the famous Feather Scroll for an exterior pattern. Typically, the shallower the bowl, the more money it brings with the purple bringing many times the price of the underrated marigold.

Butterfly Bower

Butterfly

Butterfly Tumbler

Butterfly and Berry

Butterfly and Corn Vase

Butterfly and Fern

Butterfly and Tulip

BUTTERFLY ORNAMENT

I'm told this interesting bit of glass was made as a give-away item and attached to bon-bons, baskets and compotes by a bit of putty when purchasers visited the Fenton factory. This would certainly explain the scarcity of the Butterfly ornament for few are around today. Colors I've heard about are marigold, amethyst, cobalt blue, ice blue, white and green.

BUTTERFLY PINTRAY

While most of these are seen in marigold, often pale and washed out, this example is the pastel version with pink wings and blue body and is a richly iridized beauty. It measures 8″ across and is 7″ tall. These were made by the same company that made the Tall Hats.

BUTTERMILK GOBLET

Exactly like the Iris goblet also made by Fenton, the plainer Buttermilk Goblet is a real beauty and rather hard to find, especially in green or amethyst. As you can see, the iridescence is on the interior of the goblet only, and the stem is the same as the Fenton Vintage compotes.

BUTTON AND DAISY HAT

Again, here is an item that has been reproduced in every type of glass known, but the example shown is old and original, and has resided in one of the major Carnival glass collections in the country for many years. Like so many of the miniature novelty items, the coloring is a beautiful clambroth with lots of highlights. Manufacturer unknown.

BUZZ SAW CRUET

This eagerly hunted Cambridge novelty always brings top dollar when it comes up for sale. Found in two sizes, the colors seen are green and marigold. The mold work is fantastic as is the iridescence. Oddly, the base shows a pontil mark indicating the cruet was blown into a mold. Normally, the Buzz Saw Cruet was sold with a matching glass stopper, but the one shown (like so many around today) has long since lost the stopper. Again, these were probably designed as containers for some liquid, but just what, we can't say.

CACTUS (MILLERSBURG)

This Rays and Ribbons exterior reminds me of the famous Hobstar and Feather pattern with its incised fans, edged with needles and the hobstars above. In addition, there is a small file filler near the base, merging into a diamond where the feathers meet.

CAMBRIDGE #2351

This Cambridge near-cut pattern was made in a host of shapes in crystal, but in iridized glass only the punch set pieces and a bowl have been reported so far. The punch set was advertised in marigold, amethyst and green, and the one reported bowl is also green.

CANDLE VASE

While I know nothing about this unusually shaped vase except that it is 9½″ tall, I can say with some certainty it was probably shaped in several other ways in many instances. I haven't had any other colors reported, but they may exist.

CANE

One of the older Imperial patterns, Cane is found on wine goblets, bowls of various sizes and pickle dishes. The coloring is nearly always a strong marigold, but the bowl has been seen on smoke, and I'm sure amethyst is a possibility. Cane is not one of the more desirable Imperial patterns and is readily available, especially on bowls; however, a rare color would improve the desirability of this pattern.

Cactus (Millersburg)

Cambridge #2351

Butterfly Pintray

S-Band Exterior

Butterfly Ornament

Button and Daisy Hat

Buzz Saw Cruet

Candle Vase

Buttermilk Goblet

Cane

CANE AND SCROLL (SEA THISTLE)
I'd guess there are other shapes around in this pattern, but the small creamer shown is the only one I've seen so far. As you can see, there are four busy patterns competing with one another but their combination isn't unattractive. The marigold has a reddish hue.

CANNON BALL VT.
While the shape of this Fenton water set is the same as the Cherry and Blossom usually found in cobalt, this marigold version has a much different enameled design. The tumblers have an interior wide panel design, and I'm sure this is quite a scarce item.

CAPTIVE ROSE
Captive Rose is a very familiar decorative pattern found in bowls, bon-bons, compotes and occasional plates in colors of marigold, cobalt blue, green, amethyst, amber and smoke. The design is a combination of embroidery circles, scales and diamond stitches and is a tribute to the mold maker's art. The roses are like finely stitched quilt work. Manufactured by Fenton.

CARNIVAL BEADS
I have always resisted showing strands of beads before, even though they are very collectible and quite attractive. but when Lee Briix sent this very interesting photo using a Rustic vase as a prop, I changed my mind. most of these beads were made in smaller glass factories or in Europe.

CAROLINA DOGWOOD
This very interesting Westmoreland pattern is rather hard to find and the few examples I've seen have all been on milk glass base with either a marigold lustre or a beautiful bright auqua finish. The design is fairly good, featuring a series of six dogwood sprays around the bowl with a single blossom in the center. Simple but effective.

CARTWHEEL COMPOTE
Not only is this flash-iridized compote marked, it is marked twice - on the base and on the bowl. The color is pale as are most items from the Heisey Company, but quite pretty.

CATHEDRAL (CURVED STAR)
After years of uncertainty and guessing, we've traced this pattern to Sweden and the Eda Glassworks. Several shapes exist including a chalice, pitcher, bowl, flower holder, epergne, compote, butterdish, creamer, open sugar, two-piece fruit bowl, and a rare rose-bowl. Colors are marigold and blue.

CENTRAL SHOE STORE
Perhaps this is one of the more scarce Northwood advertising pieces and like most it is a shallow bowl, nearly 6″ in diameter. Its lettering says: "Compliments of the Central Shoe Store - Corner of Collinsville and St. Louis Avenues - East St. Louis, Illinois." The floral sprays are much like others used on similar pieces from the Northwood Company.

Central Shoe Store

Carnival Beads

38

Cane and Scroll

Cannon Ball Vt.

Captive Rose

Carolina Dogwood

Cartwheel Compote

Cathedral (Curved Star)

CHATELAINE

Most of the authorities in the field agree this very rare, beautiful water set pattern is an Imperial item. I'm listing it as a questionable one, however, because I've seen no proof of its origin. Of course, I can't emphasize too strongly its quality or scarcity, and the selling price on the few examples to be sold publicly verify this. The only color I've heard of is a deep rich purple.

CHECKERBOARD

It has been pretty well established that Checkerboard was a Westmoreland product which partially explains its rarity today. I've seen about half a dozen tumblers over the years but the pitcher shown is one of only three known to exist. The color, iridescence and mold-work are outstanding. A rare goblet is occasionally found iridized.

CHERRY (DUGAN)

Almost every Carnival glass company produced one or more cherry patterns, and for many years the Dugan Cherry was much confused with the Millersburg Cherry pattern. Of course, there is a considerable difference on comparison and much of the confusion has now been dispelled. The Dugan version is confined to bowls, flat or footed. It has fewer cherries on the branches, no stippling on the branches and less detailed veining on the leaves. The exterior pattern (if there is one) is often Jeweled Heart.

CHERRY (MILLERSBURG)

For many years, Northwood was credited with this beautiful pattern (much as the Fenton company had been for the "Poinsettia" bowl we now know was made by Northwood) but in recent years this error has been rectified. To be sure, the Northwood company did make two Cherry patterns, but the Millersburg Cherry is easily distinguished from either of these since it has more cherries in the clusters, greater variety in the leaf design and appears to be almost "drooping" in appearance.

CHERRY AND CABLE

Sometimes called "Cherry and Thumbprint," this is a very difficult Northwood product to locate, and to date I've seen one tumbler, one pitcher, a table set and a small berry bowl. The pattern is very much a typical Northwood design and reminds one of the famous Northwood Peach, especially in the shape of the butter dish bottom which carries the same exterior base pattern as the Prisms compote. I know of no colors except a good rich marigold, but others may certainly exist.

CHERRY CHAIN

Cherry Chain is a close relative of the Leaf Chain pattern shown elsewhere in this book. Found on bowls, plates and bon-bons, this all-over pattern is well done and effective. The colors are marigold, blue, green, amethyst and white. There is an extremely rare example of this pattern on a red slag base glass, and it is the only one I've heard about. There is a variant also.

Chatelaine

Checkerboard Water Set

Cherry (Dugan)

Cherry (Millersburg)

Cherry and Cable

Cherry Chain

41

CHERRY CIRCLES

This Fenton piece employs a pattern of fruit combined with a scales pattern, the latter being a favorite filler device at the Fenton factory. Cherry Circles is best known in large bon-bons, but compotes, bowls and occasional plates do exist in marigold, cobalt blue, green, amethyst, white and red.

CHERRY/HOBNAIL (MILLERSBURG)

On comparison, the interior cherry design varies enough from the regular Millersburg Cherry to show this separate example with the hobnail exterior. These bowls are quite rare and are found in marigold, amethyst and blue and measure roughly 9″ in diameter. A 5″ bowl can also be found, both with and without the hobnail exterior.

CHRISTMAS COMPOTE

Some dispute has arisen over the origin of this large and beautiful compote, and while some declare it a Millersburg product, I'm inclined to believe it came from the Northwood factory. It is rare and available in both purple and marigold.

CHRYSANTHEMUM

For years I thought this might be an Imperial pattern for it so reminded me of the Windmill pattern, but it really is Fenton. Found on large bowls, either footed or flat, Chrysanthemum is known in marigold, blue, green, ice green, white and a very beautiful red.

CHRYSANTHEMUM DRAPE LAMP

This beauty would grace any glass collection. As you can see, the font is beautifully iridized and has been found in pink glass as well as white. Strangely, most of these lamps have been found in Australia, but the maker is thus far unknown.

CIRCLE SCROLL

Dugan's Circle Scroll is not an easy pattern to find, especially in the water sets, hat shape and vase whimseys. Other shapes known are berry sets, compotes, creamers and spooners. The colors I've seen are marigold and purple, but certainly others may exist with cobalt a strong possibility.

CLASSIC ARTS

What an interesting pattern this is. It is available in a covered powder jar, a rosebowl, a 7″ celery vase, and a rare 10″ vase. The design is very "Greek" in feeling and the tiny figures quite clear. The green paint gives an antiquing effect which adds greatly to the beauty. It was made in Czechoslovakia.

Cherry/Hobnail (Millersburg)

Cherry Circle

Christmas Compote

Chrysanthemum

Chrysanthemum Drape Lamp

Circle Scroll

Classic Arts

43

CLEVELAND MEMORIAL TRAY

Undoubtedly made to celebrate Cleveland's centennial birthday, this cigar ash tray depicts the statue of Garfield, his tomb in Lake View cemetery, the Soldiers and Sailors Monument, the Superior Street viaduct and the Cleveland Chamber of Commerce building. The coloring and iridescence are typically Millersburg, and the mold work compares favorably with that of the Courthouse bowl. A real treasure for any glass collector. Found also in amethyst.

COAL BUCKET (U.S. GLASS)

These rather rare little match holders can be found in both marigold and green and are a miniature collector's dream come true. Few are around, and they bring high prices when sold.

COBBLESTONES

This simple Imperial pattern is not often seen, but certainly is a nice item when encountered. Found on bowls of various sizes - often with Arcs as an exterior pattern. Cobblestones is also found on handled bon-bons where a beautiful radium finish is often present, and the exterior is honeycombed! A curious circumstance to say the least! The colors are marigold, green, blue, amethyst and amber. There is also a varient, as well as a rare plate.

COIN DOT (FENTON)

This pattern is fairly common on medium size bowls but can sometimes be found on plates and a handled basket whimsey. The colors are marigold, cobalt blue, green, amethyst and red, but not all shapes are found in all colors. The bowl and rosebowl are the only shapes reported in red.

COIN DOT (WESTMORELAND)

Once these were all thought to be made only by the Fenton Company. The variations and some timely research have disclosed that the rosebowl shown, as well as a compote shape and bowl the rosebowl was pulled from, are from the Westmoreland plant. Colors are marigold, amethyst, green, milk-glass iridized, blue milk-glass iridized, teal and aqua opalescent.

COIN SPOT

This undistinguished little Dugan compote holds a dear spot in my heart for it was the first piece of Carnival glass we ever owned. Made in opalescent glass also, in Carnival glass it is found in marigold, green, purple, peach, white and blue. The design is simple consisting of alternate rows of indented stippled ovals and plain flat panels. The stem is rather ornate with a finial placed mid-way down. Often in marigold, the stem remains clear glass.

COLONIAL

Imperial's Colonial pattern is simply one version of wide panelling. The shapes I've heard about are vases, toothpick holders, open sugars, candlesticks and the handled lemonade goblet shown. Colors are marigold, green and purple, usually of the very rich nature.

Coal Bucket (U.S. Glass)

Cleveland Memorial Tray

Cobblestone

Coin Dot

Coin Dot Rosebowl

Coin Spot

Colonial

COLONIAL LADY

Just look at the color on this rare vase! It certainly rivals Tiffany and only proves Imperial was topped by no one in purple glass. Colonial Lady stands 5¾" tall and has a base diameter of 2¾". I've heard of no other color, except marigold, but certainly others may exist. Needless to say, these are not plentiful.

COLONIAL VARIANT

Perhaps this isn't really a variant, but with the lid, it looks different. It was made by Imperial and is found in marigold and sometimes clear Carnival.

COLUMBIA

Made first in crystal, Columbia is found in Carnival glass on compotes and vase shapes, all from the same mold. The coloring is usually marigold, but amethyst and green are known. While the simplicity of Columbia may not be appreciated by some collectors, it certainly had its place in the history of the glass field and should be awarded its just dues. Manufactured by Imperial. Shown is a rare rosebowl whimsey.

CONCAVE DIAMOND

Most of us have seen the Concave Diamond water sets in ice blue and tumblers in vaseline, but I hadn't seen another shape until encountering this quite rare pickle caster in a beautiful marigold. That brought back a memory of finding a small fragment of this pattern in the Dugan shards from the 1975 Indiana, Pennsylvania, diggings, so I would speculate this rare item originated at that factory. Also known are "tumble-ups" in aqua, marigold and aqua opalescent.

CONCAVE FLUTE (WESTMORELAND)

This rather plain pattern is attributed to the Westmoreland Company and is found as shown, on rosebowls and pulled out into a vase shape. Colors I've heard about are marigold, amethyst and green but certainly aqua is a possibility.

CONCORD

Even among all the other grape patterns in iridized glass, I'm sure you won't confuse Concord with the others, for the netlike filler that coves the entire surface of the bowls' interior is unique. Found in both bowls and plates, Concord is a very scarce Fenton pattern and is available in marigold, green, amethyst, blue and amber. It is a collector's favorite and doesn't sell cheaply.

CONE AND TIE

The simple beauty of this very rare tumbler (no pitcher is known of now) is very obvious; and while most collectors credit it to Imperial, I cannot verify its maker. The coloring is a very outstanding purple on the few examples known, and the selling price only emphasizes its desirability. Rarely does one of these move from one collection to another.

CONSTELLATION

Constellation is a seldom seen compote, rather smaller than most. It measures 5" tall and has a bowl diameter that averages 5½" across. The exterior pattern is called Seafoam and I've seen this compote in peach opal, a strange white, over yellow (vaseline) glass and white Carnival. It was made by Dugan.

COOLEEMEE, N.C.

This 9" Advertising Heart and Vine plate is a rare one. Only four or five are known and all are marigold. The plate was sold to promote the J. N. Ledford textile mill company of Cooleemee, North Carolina and undoubtedly was a give-away item. Today it is a rare and valuable collector's item. Of course, it was made by Fenton.

Concave Flute (Westmoreland)

Cooleemee, N.C.

Colonial Lady

Colonial Variant

Concave Diamond

Concord

Cone and Tie

Constellation

Columbia

47

CORAL

I'd guess the same designer who gave us the Peter Rabbit and Little Fishes pattern is also responsible for Coral; the bordering device for all three is almost identical. Coral is found in bowls mostly, but a rare plate and rarer compote are known in various colors, including marigold, blue, green, vaseline and white. Manufactured by Fenton.

CORINTH

Long attributed to Northwood, Corinth is another pattern from the Dugan factory. It is found on bowls, vases and the beautiful banana dish shown, in marigold, green, amethyst, and peach opalescent. The example shown is 8¼" long and is iridized on the inside only. A variant is credited to Westmoreland.

CORN BOTTLE

Perhaps the Corn Bottle is not an Imperial product, but the beautiful helios green has always made me feel it was, so while I list it as a questionable Imperial product, I stand convinced it is. Colors found are marigold, green, amethyst and smoke (another indication Imperial made it), all of good quality. The iridescence is usually outstanding as is the moldwork. It stands 5" tall and usually has a cork stopper.

CORN CRUET

Since I first saw this years ago, I've been able to learn little about it. The only color reported is the white. Rumor places it in the Dugan line, but I can't be sure.

CORN VASE

This is one of the better known Northwood patterns, and that's little wonder because it is such a good one. Usually about 7" tall, there are certain variants known; especially noteworthy is the rare "pulled husk" variant that was made in very limited amounts. The colors are marigold, green, purple, ice blue, ice green and white. The mold-work is outstanding, the color superior and the glass fine quality - truly a regal vase.

CORNING INSULATOR

While I've never been very excited by insulators, this one has super color and is marked "Corning - Reg. USA Pat.". It is only one of several sizes that can be found.

CORONATION (VICTORIAN CROWN)

This bulbous vase shape stands 5" tall and measures 3" across the lip. It has four Victorian crowns around and suspended coronets between. It is, of course, English, but from what company I can't say, not can I pin down its use except to call it a vase shape.

COSMOS

Green seems to have been the only color in this Millersburg pattern, and small bowls abound; however, an occasional 7" plate can be found. The radium finish is spectacular, and the mold work is outstanding.

COSMOS AND CANE

What a mystery this pattern has always been to me! Made in white and a soft honey-marigold shade, the shapes are numerous including a berry set, a table set, a water set, a rose bowl, a chop plate, a rare tall compote, a shorter compote and several whimsey shapes. In the whimseys, a rare amethyst color can be found. Shown is a rare oval plate.

Corning Insulator

Corn Cruet

48

Corinth

Coral

Corn Bottle

Coronation (Victorian Crown)

Corn Vase

Cosmos

Cosmos and Cane

COSMOS VT.

Cosmos Variant is a Fenton pattern found in bowls and occasionally plates (a compote has been reported but I haven't seen it). Amethyst is probably the most available color, but Cosmos Variant can be found in marigold, purple, blue, white, iridized milk glass and red.

COUNTRY KITCHEN

Used as both a primary and secondary pattern, this hard-to-come-by design is quite artistic. The berry sets are next to impossible to locate, and the four piece table sets are quite scarce and expensive. These, of course, are all primary uses; however, County Kitchen is more often seen as an exterior pattern on the lovely Fleur-de-lis bowls where it compliments the latter perfectly. Millersburg seemed to have a flair for creating outstanding near-cut patterns, and this is certainly one of them. A variant is called Potpourri.

COURTHOUSE

Frankly, I wasn't greatly impressed by the first of these I saw. I'm not quite sure what I'd expected but perhaps it was the smallness of the bowl that disappointed me. Now, however, I wouldn't part with my Courthouse bowl, and I find my admiration for it growing each time I look at it. Known in two shapes - plain or ruffled - and two variations - lettered or unlettered - this 7″ shallow bowl typifies the Millersburg technique. The mold work is sharp and detailed, and the glass is very fine and transparent. These things, added to the radium finish, spell quality - a rare thing for a piece of souvenir glass, and points out the John Fenton flair for quality regardless of cost.

COVERED HEN (CHIC)

The Covered Hen is probably the best recognized piece of English Carnival glass made at the Sowerby Works. Known in a good rich marigold as well as a weak cobalt blue, the Covered Hen is 6⅞″ long. The mold work is very good but the color ranges from very good to poor. While reproductions have been reported, my British sources tell me this isn't true, and that no examples have been made since the 1940's.

COVERED FROG

These very realistic covered pieces are 5½″ long and stand about 4″ tall. They are found in marigold, white, ice blue and the very natural ice green shown. All colors are rare, especially the marigold.

COVERED SWAN

This beautiful English pattern is a companion to the Covered Hen and can be found in both marigold and amethyst. It measures 7¾″ long and as you can see, the neck doesn't touch the back! What a mold maker's achievement! The base is identical to that of the covered Hen dish. Both are butter dishes.

CRAB CLAW

Crab Claw is indeed a curious near-cut pattern that very seldom enters discussions by collectors, but isn't as readily found as many other geometrics from the Imperial Company. Found on bowls of various sizes, a two piece fruit bowl and base, and scarce water sets, the pattern is most often found in marigold, but amethyst and green are known in the bowl shapes. The design features hobstars, curving file and diamond devices, and daisy-cut half-flowers, all seemingly interlocking.

Covered Frog

Cosmos Vt.

Country Kitchen

Courthouse

Covered Hen

Covered Swan

Crab Claw

CRACKLE

Crackle is very common, very plentiful pattern available in a large variety of shapes, including bowls, covered candy jars, water sets, auto vases, punch sets, plates, spittoons and a rare window ledge planter. Marigold is certainly the most found color, but green and amethyst do exist on some shapes. And often the color and finish are only adequate. Crackle was mass produced in great amounts, probably as a premium for promotional giveaways, so I suppose we can't expect it to equal other Carnival items.

CRUCIFIX

Now known to be from the Imperial Glass Company, these rare candlesticks are known in marigold Carnival glass and crystal. The Crucifix candlestick is 9½″ tall and is very heavy glass.

CRYSTAL CUT

This beautiful compote comes to us from Australia and as you can see, is a very nice geometric design. Other colors and shapes may exist, but if so, I haven't seen them. It measures 7″ in diameter.

CURVED STAR (CATHEDRAL)

Here is another view of this Swedish pattern. Shown is the base of the fruit set which, upended, makes a nifty compote as you can see. It is probably used more often in this capacity than its original purpose.

CUT ARCHES

While I'm fairly confident this is another geometric pattern of English origin, I can't remember even seeing another shape in this pattern. As you can see, it is a banana boat of quite heavy glass. The only color reported is the marigold shown, and it has the typical marigold look of English glass. The deeply cut design would certainly lend itself to a waterset.

CUT COSMOS

How I wish I knew who made this beautiful tumbler! The design is top-notch and certainly deserves full recognition, but the maker remains unknown. The only color reported is the marigold shown, and it has the typical marigold look of English glass. The deeply cut design would certainly lend itself to a waterset.

CUT FLOWERS

Here is one of the prettiest of all the Jenkins' patterns. Standing 10½″ tall, the intaglio work is deep and sharp and the cut petals show clear glass through the luster, giving a beautiful effect. Most Cut Flowers vases are rather light in color, but the one shown has a rich deep marigold finish. Cut Flowers can also be found in a smoke color.

Cut Arches

Crackle

Crucifix

Crystal Cut

Curved Star

Cut Cosmos

Cut Flowers

CUT OVALS

This Fenton pattern falls into the stretch glass field, but because of the etching it is considered Carnival glass. Known in both candlesticks and bowls, Cut Ovals can be found in marigold, smoke, ice blue, ice green, pink, white, tangerine, lavender, red and vaseline. The candlesticks are 8½″ tall and the bowls are known in 7″, 8″, 9″ and 10″ sizes.

DAHLIA

Make no mistake, Dahlia is an important, often scarce, always expensive, Dugan pattern. The glass is fine quality, the design highly raised and distinct, and the iridescence super. Found only in marigold, purple and white, Dahlia is made only in berry sets, table sets, and water sets, all useful shapes, which probably explains the scarcity due to breakage in use. The water sets are much sought.

DAISY

Found only in the bon-bon shape, Fenton's Daisy pattern is very scarce. The pattern is a simple one of four strands of flowers and leaves around the bowl and one blossom with leaves in the center. While marigold has been reported, blue is the color most found, and although I haven't seen amethyst or green they may exist.

DAISY AND CANE

This rare little decanter is a very unusual design, seldom seen. The coloring is typical of English marigold and has quite good iridescence. I've never seen the stopper so can't verify what it is like. The decanter stands 8″ tall and has a 3½″ base diameter. I suspect that Sowerby's made this, but can't say positively.

DAISY AND DRAPE

This pattern is probably a spin-off of the old U.S. Glass pattern, "Vermont," the main difference being the standing row of daisies around the top edge. Made in most of the Northwood colors, the purple leads the vivid colors, while the aqua opalescent is the most sought of the pastels. White is probably the most available color, but even it brings top dollar.

DAISY AND PLUME

Daisy and Plume is an exterior pattern found on the large Northwood Blackberry compotes as well as the primary pattern of its own compotes and footed rosebowls. It is, of course, a very adaptable pattern and could be used on many shapes. One wonders why it does not appear on table sets or water sets, but unfortunately this is the case. The colors are marigold, white, purple, electric blue, green, peach, and aqua.

Cut Ovals

Dahlia

Daisy

Daisy and Cane

Daisy and Drape

Daisy and Plume

DAISY BASKET

Like many other of the Imperial handled baskets in shape and size, the Daisy Basket is a large hat shaped one with one center handle that is rope patterned. The basket stands 10½″ tall to the handle's top and is 6″ across the lip. The colors are a good rich marigold and smoke, but be advised this is one of the shapes and patterns Imperial reproduced in the 1960's.

DAISY BLOCK ROWBOAT

Originally used as a pen tray in crystal, this Sowerby product had a matching stand, but I've never seen the stand in Carnival. Daisy Block was made in marigold, amethyst, and aqua in iridized glass. It measures 10½″ in length.

DAISY CUT BELL

What a joy this very scarce Fenton pattern is. It was called a "tea bell" in a 1914 catalog, and as you can see, the handle is clear and scored and the Daisy design is all intaglio. The Daisy Cut Bell stands 6″ tall and is found in marigold only. It is a four mold design and has a marking inside "PATD APPLD."

DAISY SQUARES

When I first showed this pattern in my Millersburg book 15 years ago, I truly believed it came from that company, but over the years I've grown skeptical. At any rate, it can be found in compotes, rosebowls and goblets, all from the same mould and in marigold, amethyst, a light airey green and a strange amber base glass with over coloring of green.

DAISY WEB

What a hard-to-find pattern this is. Only the hat shape is known, and the only colors I've seen are amethyst, blue and marigold. From the exterior design of Beaded Panels we know this pattern came from the Dugan company, so peach is definite possibility.

DAISY WREATH

Apparently Westmoreland decided this pattern looked best on a milk glass base for I haven't heard of it any other way. The 9″ bowl in marigold on milk glass is quite scarce. Equally scarce is the aqua blue on milk glass shown.

DANCE OF THE VEILS

I've heard of three of these beauties by the Fenton Company in iridized glass, and they are truly a glassmaker's dream. Marigold is the only Carnival color although crystal, pink, green, custard and opalescent ones are made.

Daisy Web

Daisy Basket

Daisy Block Rowboat

Daisy Cut Bell

Daisy Squares

Daisy Wreath

Dance of the Veils

DANDELION

I have serious misgivings about labeling both of the pictured items as the same pattern, but since this is how they are best known, I will yield to tradition. Actually, the mug is certainly a dandelion pattern that is quite rare and popular, especially in aqua opalescent. Occasionally a mug bears advertising on the base and is called the "Knight Templar" mug; it brings top dollar!

The water set, while known as Dandelion, is not the same design, but nonetheless is an important Northwood pattern. It is found in marigold, purple, green, ice blue, white and a very rare ice green. The tankard pitcher is regal.

DEEP GRAPE COMPOTE

Ever notice how few compotes were made by Millersburg? This is one of the rarer ones, found in cobalt, amethyst, green, marigold and vaseline. It stands about 7″ high and the stem is panelled. The grape clusters and leaves are richly detailed and the mold work is outstanding.

DIAMOND AND DAISY CUT

This beautiful pattern is found on 10″ vases, compotes and rare water sets (which have been mistakenly labeled Mayflower). Found primarily in a good rich marigold, the compote has been in amethyst so perhaps other colors exist.

DIAMOND AND FAN (MILLERSBURG)

This is a beautifully designed exterior pattern, always found with the Nesting Swan bowl in Carnival glass. As you can see, the pattern literally covers all available space but doesn't seem busy.

DIAMOND AND FILE

I'm not at all sure this pattern is Imperial, but list it here as a possible one. It hasn't a great deal of imagination, but may have been intended as give-aways or quick sales. The small bowl shown is quite deep, possibly intended as a jelly holder. The color is adequate, and I've heard of these in smoke as well as marigold.

DIAMOND AND RIB

Diamond and Rib is a Fenton pattern that has caused great confusion in the collecting world. This is because the jardiniere shape was long suspected to be a Millersburg product. This size has been found in large vases just like the smaller ones, so that we know there were two sizes of molds used. Colors are marigold, green, amethyst, smoke and blue.

DIAMOND AND SUNBURST

Known in bowls, decanters, goblets and the rare oil cruet shown, Diamond and Sunburst is an Imperial pattern. Colors are marigold, green, purple and amber.

Diamond And Fan (Millersburg)

Dandelion

Deep Grape Compote

Diamond and Daisy Cut

Diamond and File

Diamond and Rib

Diamond and Sunburst

59

DIAMOND FLUTES

This pattern is shown in a 7¼" parfair glass. The coloring is a good marigold at the top, running to clear at the base. Other shapes are not reported but may exist.

DIAMOND FOUNTAIN

This beautiful cruet has now been traced to the Higbee Company and appears in their 1910 ads as a pattern called Palm Leaf Fan in crystal. As you can see, the mold work is quite good and the color adequate.

DIAMOND LACE

There seems to be a great deal of doubt about the maker of this beautiful water set and some credit it to Imperial, while others proclaim it to be a Heisey product. I personally lean toward Imperial as the maker because of the beautiful coloring, the mold sharpness and the clarity of glass. In most ways, it greatly resembles the Chatelain water set or the Zippered Heart berry set as to coloring and mold work. Diamond Lace is found in berry sets and water sets in colors of marigold and purple, but white has also been reported.

DIAMOND OVALS

Known in only two shapes thus far, a creamer on a foot and a stemmed compote, Diamond Ovals is a Sowerly product. The creamer is one of the smaller ones, measuring 4¾" tall. The only color reported is marigold, but certainly others may exist.

DIAMOND PINWHEEL

Perhaps there are other shapes in this pattern, but if so, I haven't seen them. As you can see, it is a simple geometric design, but very pleasing. The glass and luster all have good quality and certainly add to any collection.

DIAMOND POINT

While this Northwood pattern is quite typical of most vase patterns, it has a certain distinction of its own. While refraining from "busyness," it manages an interesting overall pattern. It is found in purple, blue, aqua opalescent, green, marigold, peach and white and is normally of standard height, being 10" to 11" tall.

Diamond Flutes

Diamond Fountain

Diamond Lace

Diamond Ovals

Diamond Pinwheel

Diamond Point

DIAMOND POINT COLUMNS

I haven't heard of this Imperial pattern in any other color than a good rich marigold, but that certainly doesn't mean they do not exist. The shapes known are compotes, plates, vases, table sets, and powder jars (which are rare). While the design of alternating rows of plain and checkered panels is quite simple, the overall appearance is quite effective. It is also found in small bowls.

DIAMOND POINTS BASKET

Although the dimensions are nearly the same as Northwood's Basket, the Diamond Points Basket is a much rarer pattern. And while some collectors have credited the Fenton Company with this much sought novelty, I lean toward Northwood as the maker. The colors found are marigold, purple and a radiant cobalt blue. The mold work is sharp and precise and the iridescence heavy and outstanding. I have heard of less than a dozen of these baskets, so lucky are you if you own one.

DIAMOND PRISMS

I've seen this same compote shaped with the sides squared, and it was also on the same shade of marigold with much amber in the tint.

DIAMOND RING

This typical geometric design of file fillers, diamonds and scored rings is found on berry sets as well as a fruit bowl of larger dimensions. The usual colors of marigold and smoke are to be found and in addition, the fruit bowl has been reported in a beautiful deep purple. While Diamond Ring is not an outstanding example of the glass maker's art, it certainly deserves its share of glory. Manufactured by Imperial.

DIAMONDS

Most collectors are familiar with this pattern in the water sets but it does appear on rare occasions in a punch bowl and base (no cups have yet come to light). Like its cousin, Banded Diamonds, the design is simple but effective. The glass and iridescence are very good and all have the "Millersburg look."

DIVING DOLPHINS (ENGLISH)

For many years, this scarce item was credited to the Imperial Company, but we know now it was a Sowerly product. The interior carries the Scroll Embossed pattern, and Diving Dolphins is found in marigold, blue, green and amethyst with the latter easiest to find. It measures 7″ across the bowl and may be round, ruffled, turned in like a rosebowl, or five-sided.

Diamond Point Columns

Diamond Points Basket

Diamond Prisms

Diamond Ring

Diamonds

Diving Dolphins

DOGWOOD SPRAYS

This is a pattern so very familiar to all Carnival collectors, for there are probably more bowls with various floral sprays than any other design. Dogwood Sprays, while well done, is not extraordinary in any sense of the word. Found on both bowls and compotes, the color most seen is peach but purple does turn up from time to time. Manufactured by Dugan.

DOLPHINS COMPOTE

If I had to pick my very favorite Millersburg pattern, this would be it hands down. Not only is it unique in the entire field of Carnival glass by virtue of its exterior design, but combined with the Rosalind interior, an almost perfect coordination is brought about. It simply looks good from any angle. Add to this the fine coloring and the radium finish and the Dolphins Compote is a true work of art, one that any company could be proud of.

DOUBLE DOLPHIN

Some people will probably question this pattern appearing here for it is rightly considered stretch glass, but the mold work of the dolphins tend to bridge the gap between the stretch and Carnival glass so I've shown it here. This Fenton pattern was made in many shapes, including bowls, compotes, vases, covered candy dishes, candlesticks and cake plates. Colors are ice blue, ice green, white, pink, red, topaz, tangerine and amethyst.

DOUBLE DUTCH

While it's difficult to say whether this pattern came before or after Windmill and the NuArt plate, it is quite obvious they were all the work of the same artist. All depict various rural scenes with trees, a pond and bridge. This Imperial pattern is featured on a 9½" footed bowl, usually in marigold but occasionally found in smoke, green and amethyst. The coloring is superior and the mold work very fine. The exterior bowl shape and pattern is much like the Floral and Optic pattern.

DOUBLE FAN TUMBLER

Please notice the very appealing shape of this rare, rare tumbler (two known), for it is very balanced as is the design. And while the coloring is only so-so, the glass is very clear and the mold work excellent. The Double Fan tumbler stands 3¾" tall and is 2½" across the diameter of the base. Certainly a complete water set would be a treasure indeed, regardless of the manufacturer.

DOUBLE LOOP

This Northwood pattern is found on creamers, as shown, and an open sugar with a stem. Often these are trademarked, but not all are. The colors known are marigold, green, purple, aqua opalescent and cobalt with the latter most difficult to find.

Dogwood Sprays

Dolphins Compote

Double Dolphin

Double Dutch

Double Fan Tumbler

Double Loop

DOUBLE SCROLL

The Double Scroll pattern was Imperial's try at an Art Deco pattern in iridized glass and can be found on candlesticks' a dome-based console bowl, and a punch cup in marigold, green, amethyst, smoke and red (not all colors in all shapes). The candlesticks measure 8½" tall and the oval shaped console bowl that went with them is 10½" by 8½" in diameter and stands 5" tall. The scrolls are of solid glass. The glass is thick and fine and the coloring is excellent.

DOUBLE STAR

In reality, this is the same pattern as the Buzz Saw cruet, but for some reason it has been called by this different name. Found in water sets and a rare spittoon whimsey formed from a tumbler, this Cambridge pattern is seen mostly in green, but marigold and amethyst can be found. I consider Double Star one of the best designed water sets in all of Carnival glass.

DOUBLE STEM ROSE

Like other patterns made at the Dugan plant, this pattern has mistakenly been attributed to the Fenton Company. Double Stem Rose is found on dome-footed bowls of average size in marigold, blue, green, lavender, amethyst and white. The design is interesting and well executed.

DRAGON AND BERRY (STRAWBERRY)

Obviously a companion piece to well known Dragon and Lotus pattern, Dragon and Berry apparently didn't have the popularity of its cousin for few examples are to be found. Known in both footed and flat based bowls and in colors of marigold, green, and blue, this Fenton pattern is a much sought item.

DRAGON AND LOTUS

Probably one of the best known of all Carnival glass patterns, Dragon and Lotus was a favorite of all Fenton patterns produced over several years. Shapes are flat or footed bowls and rare plates. Colors are marigold, green, blue, amethyst, peach opalescent, iridized milk glass, aqua opalescent, vaseline opalescent, red and the pastels.

DRAGON'S TONGUE

Known mostly in light shades in a milk glass with marigold iridescence, Dragon's Tongue is also found on a large footed bowl that has a diameter measurement of 11". The only color reported on the bowl shape is marigold, but certainly other colors are possible, especially Fenton's famous cobalt blue.

Double Scroll

Double Star

Double Stem Rose

Dragon and Berry

Dragon and Lotus

Dragon's Tongue

DRAPERY

This is a very graceful Northwood pattern, especially when the vase has been pulled out and down to form a lovely candy dish. One is instantly reminded of great golds of soft satin draperies in a theater, especially in the vase shape, most of which are 10" to 11" in height. The colors are marigold, peach, blue, purple, green, ice blue and ice green. Shown is a rosebowl shape.

DUGAN'S VINTAGE VARIANT

I certainly wish we could avoid all the variants, but for the life of me, I don't know what else to call this very rare plate. It is one of five or six known, is much different in arrangement of grape clusters and the tendrils of the leaf center and the edging is different. It has a one-inch collar base and is found in amethyst as well as the marigold shown.

ELKS (FENTON)

Found in bowls, plates and the quite rare bell shapes, the Fenton Elk pieces were produced to be sold at Elk's conventions in Detroit (1910), Atlantic City (1911), and Parkersburg (1914). The colors found are a very rich cobalt blue and a sparkling emerald green with heavy lustre. Naturally the plates are more sought than the bowls and the bells are highly prized treasures.

ELKS (MILLERSBURG)

The Millersburg Elks bowl or "two-eyed elk" is the best of all the elks bowls or plates. It is somewhat larger than the Fenton pieces. The only color I've seen is a rich amethyst with beautiful radium finish. In addition to bowls, paperweights have been found.

ELKS NAPPY (DUGAN)

For many years I thought this beautiful nappy (two known) was a Millersburg product but recent information assures us it came from the Dugan factory. As you can see, it is a real beauty with stunning color and fine mould work. The only color is purple.

EMBROIDERED MUMS

Embroidered Mums is a rather busy pattern, saved from being overdone by a balancing of its parts. A close cousin to the Hearts and Flowers pattern, Em broidered Mums is found on bowls and bon-bons on a stem. Many of the pieces of this pattern carry the Thin Rib as a secondary pattern and perhaps a plate will someday be found. At least, it gives us something to hope for, because many Northwood patterns with this exterior are found in plates.

EMU

The Emu bowl is one of the better Australian patterns and is available on 4½" and 10½" bowls as well as large compotes and footed cake stands. The color most found is purple, but marigold and the amber over aqua base glass are found rarely. Some people call this pattern Ostrich, but the Ostrich lives in Africa and the Emu is an Australian bird with a similar appearance.

ENAMELED CARNIVAL GLASS

Toward the latter years of the Carnival glass "craze," patterns become simpler, and in order to give the customer something different, items (especially water sets and bowls) were marketed with hand-painted enamel work on them. Most of these were simple floral sprays, but occasionally an interesting fruit pattern emerged, like the scarce water set shown here. Today, these seem to be gaining in popularity and certainly deserve a place in Carnival glass history. This is a Northwood pattern called Enameled Grape.

Elks Nappy (Dugan)

Dugan's Vintage Variant

Drapery

Elks (Fenton)

Elks (Millersburg)

Embroidered Mums

Emu

Enameled Carnival Glass

ENAMELED PRISM BAND

This beautiful Fenton tankard water set is a standout in the series of enameled water sets. It can be found in marigold, blue, green (rarely) and a very impressive and scarce white. Also the floral work may vary slightly from one item to another.

ENGLISH HOB AND BUTTON

This pattern has been reproduced in the last few years in this country, especially on tray and bowl shapes in an odd shade of amberish marigold on very poor glass. The English version shown is another thing, however. The glass is clear and sparkling. The shapes are bowls, mostly, in marigold, green, amethyst and blue.

ENGRAVED GRAPE

This lovely etched pattern is from the Fenton factory and has been seen on many shapes including vases, candy jars, tall and squat pitchers, tumblers, juice glasses and a tumble-up. Colors are marigold and white.

ENGRAVED ZINNIA

While the engraving of tall and short-stemmed flowers is rather difficult to see, the tumbler has good lustre and the shape is quite nice. Has anyone seen the pitcher?

ESTATE MUG

This rare little mug appears to belong in the late Carnival era, but neverthless is a much-in-demand item, especially to mug collectors. Most of these mugs are souvenir items, and the one shown is no exception; it bears the inscription: "Souvenir of Gant, New York." The coloring is a pale marigold and the iridescence is only so-so. It measures 3″ tall.

FAN

Despite the fact most collectors have credited this pattern to Northwood, I'm really convinced it was a Dugan product. In custard glass it has been found with the well-known Diamond marking. Of course, many more shapes of the Fan pattern were made in custard. In Carnival glass, the availability is limited to the sauce dish and an occasional piece that is footed and has a handle.

The colors seen are marigold, peach and purple. Peach is the most availaⱨle color.

FAN-STAR (MILLERSBURG)

Except for the base, this very unusual Millersburg exterior is completely plain. The base has a very odd star, bursting into a fan of root-like fingers that match the ones on the Tulip Scroll vase exactly. The interior pattern is Zig-Zag and is found in the usual Millersburg colors.

FAN-TAIL

Fan-Tail is a pattern found on occasion as the interior design of Butterfly and Berry bowls. Actually, the design is made up of a series of peacock's tails swirling out from the center of the bowl, and while it is an interesting pattern, certainly is not a designer's success.

This Fenton pattern has been reported in marigold, cobalt blue, green and white.

FANCIFUL

Probably many collectors will challenge this pattern being attributed to Dugan, but shards from the Dugan factory were identified by this author in both marigold and purple, so here it is. Actually, if a comparison is carefully made with the Embroidered Mums, Heart and Flowers and Fancy patterns, one finds a close similarity that isn't evident on first glance. Fanciful is available on bowls and plates in colors of marigold, peach, purple and white. The familiar Big Basketweave adorns the exterior.

FANCY CUT

Much like the small creamers in design, Fancy Cut is actually the pitcher from a child's water set (tumblers to match are known in crystal). The color is a good rich marigold and the pitcher measures 4″ tall and has a base diameter of 2¼″. The design is a bit busy, combining several near-cut themes, but the rarity of the iridized version more than makes up for this.

Engraved Zinnia   **Engraved Grape**

Enameled Prism Band

English Hob and Button

Fancy Cut

Fan

Estate Mug

Fan-Star (Millersburg)

Fan-Tail

Fanciful

71

FANS

The most striking thing about this pitcher is its size; larger than a creamer but smaller than a milk pitcher. It stands 5″ tall and 7″ across the handle. The design is a series of prisms in fan shapes and the only reported color is marigold. I suspect Davisons is the maker.

FARMYARD

Most people have long felt this to be Harry Northwood's masterpiece, but with the discovery of peach opalescent and evidence that the exterior pattern (Jewelled Heart) is Dugan, Farmyard is likely to be from that company. Colors are purple, fiery amethyst, green and peach opalescent.

FASHION

Fashion is probably the most familiar geometric pattern in all of Carnival glass. It was manufactured in huge amounts over a long period of time and was originally called "402½" when first issued. The shapes are creamers, sugars, punch sets, water sets, a bride's basket, and a fruit bowl and stand. While marigold is the most often seen color, smoke, green and purple are found but are scarce. This pattern was made by Imperial. A rare red punch set was made since cups exist.

FEATHER STITCH

This pattern is a kissing cousin of the well-known Coin Dot design and as such is found on bowl shapes only, although I suspect a plate shape does exist. The colors seen are marigold, blue, green and amethyst and the bowls may vary in size from 8½″ to 10″. Feather Stitch was produced by Fenton.

FEATHER AND HEART

This fine Millersburg water set, found in green, marigold and amethyst is typical in many ways of all the Millersburg water sets. The pitcher lip is long and pulled; quite low while the rim is scalloped quite like its cousin, the Marilyn set. The glass is quite clear, rather heavy and has excellent iridescence. A little difficult to find, the pattern adds greatly to any collection.

FEATHERED FLOWERS

This pretty exterior pattern is found on the Australian Kiwi bowls. It is an intaglio pattern of swirls and stylized blossoms and is quite attractive.

Fans

Farmyard

Fashion

Feather Stitch

Feather and Heart

Feathered Flowers

FEATHERED SERPENT

At one time, this pattern was felt to be a Millersburg design, but in recent years the Fenton Company has emerged as the known manufacturer. Found only in berry sets and a very rare spittoon whimsey, Feathered Serpent is available in marigold, green, blue and amethyst and has the Honeycomb and Clover as an exterior pattern.

FEATHERS

Northwood certainly made its share of vases perhaps because they were so decorative and useful. The Feathers vase is an average example usually found in marigold, purple and green and is of average size and quality.

FENTONIA

Known in berry sets, table sets, fruitbowls and water sets, Fentonia is an interesting all-over pattern of diamonds filled with the usual Fenton fillers of scales and embroidery stitchery. Colors are marigold, blue, green and occasionally amethyst, but the pattern is scarce in all colors and is seldom found for sale. There is a variant called Fentonia Fruit.

FERN

Again we find a pattern that is sometimes combined with the well-known Northwood pattern, Daisy and Plume. Fern is usually found as an interior pattern on bowls and compotes. It is an attractive pattern but really not an outstanding one.

FERN BRAND CHOCOLATES

Like so many of the small Northwood advertising pieces, this is a treasure for collectors and a real beauty for advertising buffs. The only color is amethyst, and it measures 6¼″ across.

FERN PANELS

Like so many of the Fenton novelty pieces of Carnival glass, Fern Panels is found only on the hat shape. Not too exciting, but then it apparently had an appeal of its own then as now. The colors are the usual ones: marigold, blue, green and occasionally red.

FIELD FLOWER

Originally called "494½," this much overlooked Imperial pattern is really a little jewel. Found only on a standard size water set and a rare milk pitcher, Field Flower is found in marigold, purple, green and a very beautiful clambroth. The design, basically a flower framed by two strands of wheat on a stippled background, is bordered by double arches that edge the stippled area and continue down to divide the area into panels. All in all, this is a beautiful pattern that would grace any collection.

Fern Brand Chocolates

Feathered Serpent

Feathers

Fentonia

Fern

Fern Panels

Field Flower

FIELD THISTLE

Field Thistle is a U.S. Glass Company pattern, scarce in all shapes and colors. Shapes known are berry sets, table sets, water sets, a vase, plate and small creamer and sugar called a breakfast set. Colors most found are marigold or green, but the breakfast set is known in a beautiful ice blue so other colors may exist. The pattern is all intaglio and sometimes the marigold coloring is a bit weak.

FILE

For many years, File was designated as a product of the Columbia Glass Company, but was actually made by the Imperial Glass Company and is shown as such in their old catalogs in many shapes, including bowls, water pitchers, compotes and table sets. The colors are marigold, green, smoke and amethyst, and usually the lustre is quite good with much gold in evidence. The mold work is far above average.

FINE CUT AND ROSES

The real pleasure of this Northwood pattern is the successful combination of a realistic floral pattern with a pleasing geometric one. Of course, rosebowls have a charm all their own. Really well done mold work and super color all add to its attraction, and even though it is slightly smaller than many rosebowl patterns, it is a favorite of collectors.

FINE CUT HEART (MILLERSBURG)

Here is the back pattern of the beautiful Primrose bowl, but the one shown is something special. An experimental piece with a "goofus" finish under iridization. I've seen one other Millersburg example of this on a Peacock and Urn ice cream bowl, and it was also amethyst.

FINE CUT OVALS (MILLERSBURG)

As a companion to the Whirling Leaves pattern, Fine Cut Ovals has eight ovals, each containing two sections of fine cut and two of file. At the edges, a fan flairs from a diamond center, giving interesting contrast.

FINE PRISMS AND DIAMONDS

This large English vase stands some 13½" tall and has a hefty base diameter of nearly 4". Obviously it was intended to be used and not just a decorative item. And while the design qualities aren't impressive, the glass is of good color and luster.

FINE RIB (NORTHWOOD)

Can you imagine anything simpler? Yet the Fine Rib pattern was and is a success to the extent it was used time and time again by the Northwood company as secondary patterns and is the primary one in attractive vases like the one shown. While common in marigold and purple, the green color is a scarce one in Fine Rib.

FINE RIB VASE (FENTON)

While both Northwood and Fenton produced a Fine Rib vase pattern, there are differences in the design. On the Northwood vase, the ribbing extends all the way down on the base, while the Fenton design ends in a distinctive scalloped edge above the base. Of course, Fenton made this shape and pattern in red too.

Fine Cut Heart (Millersburg)

Fine Cut Ovals (Millersburg)

Field Thistle

File

Fine Cut and Roses

Fine Prisms and Diamonds

Fine Rib

Fine Rib Vase

FINECUT RINGS

From a set of copy-right drawings we know this pattern was made by the Guggenheim, Ltd.; Company of London in 1925. Shapes shown in the drawing, are an oval bowl, vase, footed celery, covered butterdish, creamer, stemmed sugar, round bowl, footed cake plate and covered jam jar. The only color I've seen is marigold and as you can see, the coloring, mold work and luster are outstanding.

FISH VASE

This handsome vase has finally been traced to the makers of the Zipper Stitch pattern as well as the Hand Vase and is believed to come from Czechoslovakia. I've seen only marigold, but have had both amethyst and green reported to me by a British collector.

FISHERMAN'S MUG

While I'm not completely convinced this is a Dugan pattern, it seems to be by a process of elimination. At any rate, it is much sought, and like the more rare Heron Mug, has the pattern on one side only. Colors are purple, amethyst, marigold, a rare peach opalescent and a more rare blue.

FIVE HEARTS

Like so many of the Dugan patterns in peach opalescent, Five Hearts is found only on dome footed bowls of average size. It has been estimated that 60 to 75 percent of all peach Carnival was made by this company. Personally, I'd say it would be closer to 90 percent.

FLARED WIDE PANEL ATOMIZER

I've often wondered just how many iridized patterns in atomizers there really are? Certainly it was a popular item in the days of Carnival, and each of them seem to have a charm of its own. This one, while rather plain, is a real cutie.

FLEUR DE LIS (MILLERSBURG)

Named, of course, for the stylized figures which symbolize the lily of the French royal family, this beautiful Millersburg design is found on bowls of all shapes and as an interior pattern on an occasional Hobstar and Feather punch bowl. The overall pattern is formal though well-balanced, and the quality of workmanship, iridescence and color rank with the best. Especially beautiful is the dome-footed three cornered bowl in amethyst.

FLEUR DE LIS VASE (JENKINS)

Like other Jenkins patterns, this heavy vase has a deeply intaglio pattern. It stands a stately 10½″ tall and is found on a rich marigold.

Flared Wide Panel Atomizer

Finecut Rings

Fish Vase

Fisherman's Mug

Five Hearts

Fleur De Lis

Fleur De Lis Vase

FLORAL AND GRAPE

Without question, Floral and Grape is one of the most familiar of Fenton pattern for the water sets are plentiful, especially in marigold. The only other shape is a hat whimsey pulled from the tumbler and other colors are cobalt blue, amethyst, green and a scarce white. Also, there are variations due to the wear of molds and creation of new ones. A variant is credited to the Dugan Company.

FLORAL AND OPTIC

Most people are familiar with this pattern in rather large footed bowls in marigold or clear Carnival, although it exists on rare cake plates and rose bowls, and in smoke, iridized milk glass, red, a stunning aqua, white and iridized custard glass. The pattern is quite simple, a series of wide panels edged by a border band of vining flower and leaf design. A green or amethyst bowl in Floral and Optic would be a real find in this Imperial pattern.

FLORAL AND WHEAT

Found in both stemmed bon-bons and compotes, this pattern is said to come from U.S. Glass and is one of the more often found patterns. It can be found in marigold, amethyst, blue as well as peach opalescent and the coloring is usually quite rich.

FLORENTINE

Both Fenton and Northwood made these candlesticks, and it is difficult to tell them apart. These shown are the Fenton version, however. They come in many colors including pastels and red as well as the usual Carnival glass colors.

FLOWER BLOCK

This pattern is a spin-off of the Curved Star pattern, and I'm showing it here in its entirety so collectors will be able to see the complete block as designed. Most of the ones around have lost their fancy wire base and wire arranger on the top.

FLOWER POT (BLUE)

While both Imperial and Fenton made these flower pot and saucer planters, the one shown is from the Fenton Art Glass Company. It is a beautiful ice blue and is 5″ tall and 4¾″ in diameter. The plate is 6¼″ in diameter. It has been seen mostly on pastels including pink but can also be found on marigold.

FLOWERING DILL

Once again we encounter a Fenton pattern that was chosen for the hat shape only, but Flowering Dill has a bit more to offer than some in that the design is graceful, flowing and covers much of the allowed space. Flowering Dill can be found in marigold, cobalt blue, green and red.

FLOWERING VINE

The Flowering Vine compote is indeed a very scarce Millersburg item. To date, I've heard of only two examples, one in green and one in amethyst. The compote is a large one, some 9″ high and 6½″ across. The interior pattern is one of grape-like leaves and a dahlia-like flower. The finish is a fine radium one on heavy glass.

Floral And Wheat

Florentine

Floral and Grape

Floral and Optic

Flower Block

Flower Pot

Flowering Dill

Flowering Vine

FLOWERS AND FRAMES

Here is another of Dugan's dome-footed bowls found primarily in peach opalescent, but also available in marigold as well as purple and green. The bowls vary from 8″ to 10″ depending on the crimping of the rim and usually have very sharp mold detail.

FLUFFY PEACOCK

Once thought to be a Millersburg product (it's really that pretty), Fluffy Peacock is now recognized as a Fenton product, and as such is high on the list of their best in iridized glass. Known only in water sets, Fluffy Peacock is not too difficult to find in green or marigold; however, the beautiful cobalt blue is quite scarce, and the amethyst is much sought.

MILLERSBURG FLUTE

The Millersburg Flute has one or two distinct difference from any of the other Flute patterns. One, of course, is the clarity of the base glass itself but the most pronounced is the ending of the flutes themselves plus the clover leaf base. It is found in punch sets, berry sets, vases and a rare compote.

FLUTE (NORTHWOOD)

While it is certainly true all of the major makers of Carnival glass used the Flute pattern in one way or another, apparently only Imperial and Northwood thought enough of it to make it a primary pattern. Thus we find many useful shapes in an array of colors coming from the Northwood factories - including sherbets, water sets, table sets, berry sets and even individual salt dips (an item seldom encountered in Carnival glass). The green water set is probably the rarest color and shape in this pattern.

FLUTE #3 (IMPERIAL)

After I wrote the Millersburg book, a great controversy arose around the Flute pattern I showed in a small bowl and punch set. Many people thought this was the Imperial pattern called Flute #3 (it wasn't), which I've seen only on table sets, water sets, a celery or large spooner, a small toothpick holder, a sauce bowl, a two handled toothpick holder and a different punch set (since then I've seen a very large berry bowl). The obvious difference between these two Flutes is the bottom configuration. On the Imperial version, there is a definite hexagonal effect just above the base, while the Millersburg version is either slightly curved outward in a honeycomb effect or has a curved slope from the base upward.

FLUTE AND CANE (IMPERIAL)

Found in wines, champagnes, punch cups, a milk pitcher and the water set pieces shown, this is a very scarce pattern indeed. All shapes are found in marigold, but the water pitcher is reported in white also and is much sought in either color as are the marigold tumblers.

FLUTE AND HONEYCOMB (MILLERSBURG)

Here's a better look at the 5″ bowl I showed in my first Millersburg book. You can see by the design above the base why I've renamed it rather than simply calling it a Flute Variant. Super amethyst is the only color I've seen, and it matches the Big Thistle punchbowl in color and finish.

FLUTE SHERBERT (ENGLISH)

This little cutie is signed "British" in script on the underside of the base. In size they are small, measuring 3¼″ tall and 3″ across the top. The only color reported is a good marigold of deep hue.

Flute and Cane (Imperial)

Fluffy Peacock

Flowers and Frames

Flute

Millersburg Flute

Flute and Honeycomb

Flute #3

Flute Sherbet

FLUTED SCROLLS

Perhaps this should be called a spittoon, but regardless of the name it is a very rare, one-of-a-kind product in Carnival. While often found on opalescent glass, this is the only iridized item in this pattern I've heard of. Perhaps it was a novelty a Dugan worker produced for himself. The coloring is a good amethyst with average lustre.

FOLDING FAN COMPOTE

The only shape I've seen for this Dugan pattern is the stemmed shallow compote shown. Most have the ruffled edge, and the average size is 7½″ in diameter and 4″ tall. Colors are marigold, amethyst, green and peach opalescent. The one shown has a clear base, but this isn't always the case.

FOOTED PRISM PANELS

What a nice design this pretty 10″ footed vase is! It is a Sowerly product, and the only reported colors are a good rich marigold and a scarce green. The design is a series of six panels filled with star prisms in graduating sizes. The stem base is domed and gently scalloped, giving great space to the appearance.

FOOTED SHELL

Made in two sizes 5″ and a 3″ size, this little novelty from the Westmoreland Company is a scarce item, especially in the smaller size. The shell rests on three stubby feet and the iridization is on the inside only. Colors I've seen are amethyst, green, marigold and blue. Also milk glass iridized.

FORKS

I first showed this rare cracker jar in my Rarities book as an unlisted pattern but have since learned it was called "Forks" in old Cambridge ads. The only color I've seen is a very rich green, but I wouldn't rule out marigold or amethyst.

FORMAL

I'm a wee bit skeptical about this pattern, but new evidence points to Dugan as the maker. Neverthless, it is an interesting pattern found only on the vase shaped in a jack-in-the-pulpit manner and a quite scarce hatpin holder. The colors most seen are purple and marigold, but I'm told pastels do exist. The hatpin holder stands 7¼″ tall.

FOUR FLOWERS

For many years I'v been puzzled by the origin of this beautiful design, but since peach opalescent is a prominent color, I'm satisfied it was also a Dugan product. Known in bowls and plates from 6″ to 11″, colors are purple, green, marigold, peach, blue and smoke.

FOUR FLOWERS VARIANT

With all the recent research on this pattern, I seem to grow even more confused; but for argument's sake, I'll say the theory now seems to place this pattern's maker in the Scandanavian orbit of glass making. It is a beauty, whoever made it, much prettier than the regular Four Flowers and is found in bowls, plates and a stunning salver on a metal base.

Four Flowers

Folding Fan Compote

Fluted Scrolls Footed Rosebowl

Footed Prism Panels

Footed Shell

Forks

Formal

Four Flowers Vt.

Here is a very pretty near cut pattern that really quite good on all shapes. I know of punch sets, table sets, water sets and a milk pitcher in 474, as well as a nice fluted bowl. The color is usually marigold but amethyst and green do exist in some shapes and are highly prized. The glass is heavy and clear, the coloring extra fine and the mold work superior; all making Imperial's 474 a real treat to own. Rare vases are also known.

FRENCH KNOTS

I suppose most people credit this pattern to Fenton because of the shape - a typical hat with ruffled top. The design is quite nice, however, and gracefully covers most of the space except the base. The exterior is plain but nicely iridized, and the only colors I've heard about are marigold and blue. French Knots is 4″ tall and has a base diameter of 2½″.

FROLICKING BEARS

Rare is hardly the word for this distinguished pattern, and I certainly wish I could identify the maker positively, but I can't (although I lean toward the U.S. Glass Company). The coloring is an odd gun metal luster over an olive green glass. The mold work is good but not exceptional.

To date, the Frolicking Bears tumbler has sold for more money than any other, and the pitchers rank near the top of the market.

FROSTED BLOCK

Frosted Block is a very Imperial pattern found in several shapes including bowls, creamers, sugars, compotes, plates, milk pitchers, pickle dishes and rosebowls. The color most seen is a good even marigold, but as you can see from the photo, a beautiful fiery clambroth is known in most shapes. In addition, some pieces are marked "Made in USA." These pieces are much scarcer and are well worth looking for.

FRUIT AND FLOWERS

Apparently a very close relative to the Three Fruits pattern, this is another of Northwood's floral groupings so well designed and produced. Also, there are several variations of this pattern, some with more flowers intermingled with the apples, pears and cherries, often meandering almost to the very outer edge of the glass. Again the Northwood Basketweave is the exterior pattern, and Fruits and Flowers is found on compotes with handles as well as bowls and rare plates.

MILLERSBURG FRUIT BASKET

I couldn't quite believe my eyes when I first saw this Millersburg compote. But, there is was with the exterior design and shape exactly like the Roses and Fruit Compote with an interior basketweave design and a pineapple, grapes and fruit! It was a real find, I've been grateful ever since for the privilege of photographing it. It is my belief that this compote was the original pattern design but had to be modified because of the difficult in producing the intricate design and remain in a competitive price area. At this time, four have been found. Of course, it must be classified as an extreme rarity.

FRUIT SALAD

Westmoreland seems to be the maker of this beautiful and rare punch set after years of speculating. Found in marigold, amethyst and peach opal, the design is outstanding and desirable.

Fruit Salad

474

French Knots

Frolicking Bears

Frosted Block

Fruits and Flowers

Millersburg Fruit Basket

GARDEN MUMS

Here is the Northwood design used on so many of their advertising pieces. The flat plate is 6″ across, and the the coloring is a typical amethyst. Just why these few examples were left unlettered is a mystery, but they certainly add much to any collection.

GARDEN PATH

Both the regular and the variant of this pattern are outstanding examples of pattern work, and the 11″ plate shown points this out. Colors are marigold, amethyst, peach opal and white for the regular Garden Path, and amethyst and peach for the variant.

GARLAND

Quite often you'll spot one of these nicely done footed rosebowls in cobalt blue or marigold, but the green is quite rare, and I haven't heard of an amethyst one, but I suspect it was made in that color. Made around 1911, these are shown in Fenton ads well up into the later dates of iridized glass and must have been quite popular. There are three sets of wreaths and drapery around the heavily stippled bowl.

GAY 90'S

Not only because of its extreme rarity but because the design is so very well suited for a water set is this pattern recognized as one of two or three top water sets in all of Carnival glass. In every regard, excellence of workmanship is obvious. Even the sold glass handle shows leaf veining at the top and intricate petal sliping at the base. Add to this the beautiful Millersburg finish and the clarity of superior glass, and you have a real winner - the Gay 90's water set.

GEORGE W. GETTS PLATE

Here is still another of the Northwood advertising small plates with the Garden Mums design. As you can see, this one's claim to fame is the backward "S" in Grand Rapids. Whether intentional or not, it catches the eye. Amethyst is the only reported color.

GIBSON GIRL

What a cute little toothpick holder this is despite having no pattern whatsoever! It stands 2⅜″ tall. Who made it and in what other colors I haven't a clue.

GOD AND HOME (DUGAN)

For many years, little was known about this unusual water set, except that it was found only in cobalt blue. It has a laurel wreath, a sun and rays. On one side it says: "In God We Trust" and on the other, "God Bless Our Home." This rare set is now thought to have been made at the Dugan/Diamond factory, and it is a real pleasure to show it here, thanks to the Yohes of Stuttgart.

GODDESS OF HARVEST

Goddess of Harvest is the rarest of all Fenton bowl patterns and certainly deserves all the attention it gets. I've heard of six or seven of these beauties in colors of marigold, blue and amethyst and each is highly treasured by its owner. The bowl measures about 9″ in diameter and is usually found with a candy ribbon edge.

GOLDEN CUPID

This very scarce Australian beauty is something to behold. In size it is only 5¼″ in diameter and quite shallow. The glass is clear with the cupid in guilt and a strong iridescence over the surface. It may be an ash tray, but I can't be sure. Large bowls are reported also.

George W. Getts Plate

Garden Mums

88

God and Home (Dugan)

Garden Path

Garland

Gibson Girl

Gay 90's

Goddess of Harvest

Golden Cupid

GOLDEN GRAPE

Known only in bowls or rose bowls on a collar base, this is a neatly molded item without much elaboration. The exterior is completely plain, and the only colors found are green, marigold or pastel marigold, usually with a satin finish. Golden Grape was manufactured by Dugan.

GOLDEN HARVEST

Here is another U.S. Glass pattern found mostly in marigold but occasionally seen in amethyst and reported in white. As you will notice, the wines are different from the decanter but are the proper ones, and the stopper is solid glass.

GOLDEN HONEYCOMB

This interesting Imperial pattern provides an all over design without being busy. The small bowls have odd little solid glass handles that are like the ones on the breakfast set while the plate and compote do not. The only color I've heard of is a good deep marigold with very rich iridescence. While this certainly isn't in the same class as the Dugan Honeycomb rosebowl, it is a better than average item to own.

GOLDEN OXEN

While this mug has never been one of my favorites like the Heron, it is hard enough to find so that many people want one. Taller than most mugs, the only color I've seen is the marigold.

GOLDEN WEDDING

I am very pleased to show the complete item, just as sold. Notice that the cap is still sealed, the whiskey is still inside, the labels are intact and the beautiful box, dated December 31, 1924, gives us a time frame for the bottle. Several sizes exist from a full quart down to the tiny 1/10 pint size.

GOOD LUCK

I'm very sure every Carnival glass collector is familar with this pattern since most of us have found a place for an example in our collections at one time or another. The example shown is quite unusual in that it is a true aqua blue with reddish iridescence. It is the only example I've ever seen in this exact color although the Good Luck bowls and plates are found in a very wide range colors. This piece was made by Northwood.

GOTHIC ARCHES

Unlisted up until now, this beautiful vase stands 10″ tall. The flared or morning glory style top adds to the interest as does the fine smoke coloring. The maker is unknown, but I suspect Imperial. To date other colors have not been reported but probably exist.

GRACEFUL

Once again we find a very simple pattern, so very different from most Northwood offerings in the Carnival glass field. Found mostly in marigold, occasionally a rich purple or deep emerald green vase in this pattern will surface and when one of these is found, the simple beauty of the Graceful pattern becomes obvious.

Gothic Arches   90   **Golden Oxen**

Golden Grape

Golden Harvest

Golden Honeycomb

Golden Wedding

Good Luck

Graceful

GRAND THISTLE (PANELED THISTLE)

Regardless of which of the three names you choose to call this pattern (the third is Alexander Floral), the rarity and the coloring demand attention. It was made at one (or more) of the glass factories in Finland and only in blue.

GRAPE (IMPERIAL)

Perhaps reproductions have detracted too much from this beautiful Imperial pattern for most of us, but regardless of that, it remains a beautifully designed, nicely done pattern. In fact, for sheer realism, it doesn't take a backseat to any Grape pattern! The shapes are almost endless, and the colors range from marigold to amethyst, green, smoke, clambroth and amber, all usually with a very fine lustre.

GRAPE AND CABLE (FENTON)

Yes, Fenton made a Grape and Cable pattern, and it is often hard to distinguish it from Northwood's. Fenton's contribution is found in bowls (both flat and footed), plates and large orange bowls usually with the Persian Medallion interior. Colors are marigold, green, amethyst, blue and rarely red.

GRAPE (AND CABLE), NORTHWOOD

Northwood Grape is, without question, the all-time favorite in Carnival glass. Not only did it lead the field 60 years ago, it still does today. The variety of shapes available is staggering, and the color availability large; the pastels are especially sought. Of course, this pattern usually brings top dollars, especially in the rare shapes and colors. A small spittoon sold for $7,000.00 at the Wishard auction. Whatever the undeniable appeal, this uncomplicated pattern has to be rated as the top item and entire collections of the Grape aren't uncommon.

GRAPE AND CHERRY

Known only on large bowls, this Sowerly pattern is a real beauty. The design is exterior and all intaglio and is a series of grapes and cherries separated by an unusual torch and scroll design. The base has a grape and leaf design; also intaglio. The only colors I've heard about are marigold and cobalt blue, but others may certainly exist.

GRAPE AND GOTHIC ARCHES

Made in a variety of kinds of glass including crystal, custard, gold decorated, and Carnival glass, this pattern is certainly one of the earlier grape patterns. The arches are very effective, reminding one of a lacy arbor framing the grapes and leaves. While the berry sets often go unnoticed, the water sets are very desirable and are a must for all Northwood collectors.

GRAPE ARBOR

This is an underrated pattern, especially in the large footed bowl shape which carries the same exterior pattern as the Butterfly and Tulip. Of course, the tankard water set is popular, especially in the pastel colors of ice blue, ice green and white. The marigold set seldom brings top dollar, and this is a shame since it is quite nice. The only other shape in Grape Arbor is a scarce hat shape.

Grand Thistle

Grape (Imperial)

Grape and Cable (Fenton)

Grape (and Cable), Northwood

Grape and Cherry

Grape and Gothic Arches

Grape Arbor

GRAPE DELIGHT

Here is a pattern I'm sure will bring on a few outcries, because I've often heard it declared to be a Fenton product. I'm very sure, however, that it came from the Dugan family. On close comparison with several Dugan products, the mold-work is certainly compatible. Not only does it come in the scarce nut bowl shape shown but in the more often seen rosebowl. The colors are both vivid and pastel and the most unusual feature, the six stubby feet.

GRAPE LEAVES (MILLERSBURG)

Seldom found and always costly, this rare Millersburg pattern is quite like the Blackberry, Grape and Strawberry Wreath patterns except for its rarity. The major design difference lies in the center leaf and grapes, and it is found in marigold, amethyst, green and vaseline.

GRAPE LEAVES (NORTHWOOD)

Harry Northwood must have loved this pattern, for I've never seen a poor example. The purple bowls are, almost without exception, vividly brilliant with strong color and iridescence. The ice blue is one of the prettiest items in this color I've seen and green has also been found. It is sad no other shape was chosen for the Grape Leaves pattern, but this is the case. The exterior is the familiar Wild Rose pattern with a finely stippled background.

GRAPE WREATH

This bowl might be called the "missing link" for it stands squarely between the Blackberry Wreath and the Millersburg Strawberry and seems to be a part of the series - perhaps from the same designer.

Besides the various sizes of bowls, a rare spittoon whimsey, 6″ and 10″ plates are known.

GRAPE WREATH VARIANT #1 (MILLERSBURG)

Actually, only the center design has been changed on these and as you can see, it is a stylized sunburst. I've seen several sizes of bowls with this center but it looks best on the large 10″ ice cream bowls. Colors are marigold, green, amethyst and a beautiful clambroth with much fire in the luster.

GRAPEVINE LATTICE

I personally doubt the plate is really the same pattern as the water set known by the same name but will give in to tradition and list them as one and the same. The plate and bowl could be called "Twigs" since they closely resemble the Apple Blossom Twigs pattern minus the flowers and leaves. The colors are both vivid and pastels, usually with very good iridescence. This pattern was manufactured by Dugan.

GREEK KEY

This simple continuous Northwood pattern, called Roman Key in pressed glass, is really very attractive when iridized. Actually, there are three motifs used; the Ray center pattern, the Greek Key and the Beads (in the much sought water set a fourth motif of prisms is added). Besides the water set, there are flat and footed bowls as well as plates. The colors are both vivid and pastels.

Grape Wreath Variant #1

Grape Delight

**Grape Leaves
(Millersburg)**

**Grape Leaves
(Northwood)**

Grape Wreath

Grapevine Lattice

Greek Key

95

GREEK KEY AND SCALES (NORTHWOOD)

Here's a rather nice Northwood secondary pattern usually found on dome-based bowls with the Stippled Rays varient interior. The design is crisp and does a nice job.

HAMMERED BELL

Whoever made this scarce and attractive light shade should be most proud for it is an imaginative work of art. Found only on a frosty white, the pattern is clear and distinct. The metal handle may vary in design, but all were used to suspend the bell **above** or **below** the bulb.

HANDLED VASE (IMPERIAL)

Mrs. Hartung shows this neat vase with the lip turned down, and Rose Preznick drew it cupped in like a rosebowl. But here it is in the original shape, and it is very pretty indeed. It stands about 9″ tall, and the coloring is a deep rich marigold well down before paling to a lighter shade.

HARVEST FLOWER

Here is a seldom seen pattern, found only on a pitcher and tumbler in marigold, amethyst and green on the latter and only in marigold in the pitcher. The tumblers have been reproduced in a dingy purple as well as white, so beware.

HATTIE

While there is little to be called outstanding about Hattie, it nonetheless has its own charm and has the distinction of having the same pattern on both the exterior and interior. Most often found on 8″ bowls with a collar base, it is also found in a scarce rose bowl and two sizes of plates, both of which are rare. The color most seen on this Imperial product is marigold, but green and amethyst do exist, and I've heard of both amber and smoke bowls.

HEADDRESS

Here is a pattern found in two varieties because it was made both in America and in Sweden. It is found in 9″ bowls and on compotes in marigold, green and blue.

HEART AND HORSESHOE

Yes, Fenton had a version of the Good Luck pattern, and it is much harder to find than the one Northwood produced. Note that it is simply the familiar Heart and Vine pattern with the horseshoe and lettering added. Colors are marigold and green with the marigold most prevalent and the green very hard to find.

Greek Key and Scales

Hammered Bell

Harvest Flower

Hattie

Handled Vase

Headdress

Heart and Horseshoe

HEART AND TREES
Found as an interior pattern on some of the footed Butterfly and Berry bowls, Heart and Trees is a combination of three well known Fenton standards. Colors known are marigold, green and blue but certainly others may exist.

HEART AND VINE
Apparently this was one of Mr. Fenton's favorite designs, for he used several variations of it combined with the Butterfly and Berry pattern as Stream of Hearts or on the Heart and Horseshoe pattern. The Heart and Vine pattern can be found on both bowls and plates and occasionally with advertising on the latter (the Spector plate). Colors are marigold, green, amethyst, blue and white.

HEARTS AND FLOWERS
Hearts and Flowers is an intricate pattern, like so many others favored by the Northwood company. It is found on various sizes and shapes of bowls as well as small, very graceful compotes. Apparently it was designed as a close relative of the Fanciful and Embroidered Mums patterns, perhaps by the same moldmaker. Interestingly enough, the compotes in the pattern are very similar in shape to the Persian Medallion compotes attributed to the Fenton Glass Company. Shown is a rare plate in sapphire blue.

HEAVY BANDED DIAMONDS
Perhaps designed as a companion to the Banded Diamonds water set, this beautiful Australian berry set, available in both marigold and purple, is a joy to behold. The diamonds are heavily molded and stand out below the narrow thread lines and the iridescence is very rich.

HEAVY DIAMOND
I'd always thought this pattern to be a Dugan product until this vase shape in smoke appeared, so apparently it is an Imperial product. Previously reported only in marigold, shapes known besides the vases are large bowls, creamers and sugars, but others probably are around.

HEAVY GRAPE (DUGAN)
So similar in many ways to the Millersburg Vintage bowls, this Dugan pattern does have several distinctive qualities of its own. The most obvious one is, of course, the grape leaf center with grapes around its edge. Also missing are the usual tendrils and the small leaflets, and the exterior doesn't carry a hobnail pattern but a typical near cut design.

HEAVY GRAPE (FENTON)
Once called a Fenton product, this beautiful Grape design is now known to be an Imperial pattern and is available on berry sets, nappies, custard sets and plates in three sizes. The colors on most pieces are simply spectacular and include marigold, green, purple, smoke, amber, pastel green, smokey blue and clambroth. The 11″ chop plate is highly sought and always brings top dollar when sold.

Heavy Grape (Dugan)

Heart and Trees

Heart and Vine

Heavy Banded Diamonds

Heart and Flowers

Heavy Diamond

Heavy Grape (Fenton)

HEAVY HOBNAIL

I first showed this unusual item in my rarities book. At that time, only the white version was known, but since then a spectacular purple example has been seen. These were the Fenton Rustic vases that weren't pulled or slung into the vase shape and very few are known.

HEAVY IRIS

I'm sure every collector of Carnival glass has speculated at one time or another over the maker of this beautiful pattern. Some have felt Millersburg, other Fenton. Now, however, it is with some assurance we report that a very sizeable chunk of a Heavy Iris tumbler was unearthed at the Dugan dump site in 1975 so we can declare it a Dugan pattern. The shape is, of course, a graceful tankard water set. The design is sharp and heavy, simple enough to be effective yet covering much of the available space. The colors are marigold, purple and white with purple the most desired. All in all, a beautiful set to own.

HEAVY PINEAPPLE

I feel very happy to show this Fenton rarity because it is only the second example in Carnival glass to be reported. This one is a beautiful frosty white while the other was cobalt blue. Both pieces are large 10″ bowls on three feet. The design is all exterior and heavily raised. Certainly there must be other examples of Heavy Pineapple but if so, they haven't been reported. A third marigold example is known.

HEAVY PRISMS

This beautiful celery vase stands 6″ tall and shows the quality English Carnival glass makers attained. The maker is Davisons, and the colors reported are marigold, amethyst and blue. The glass is very thick and heavy and the luster top notch.

HEAVY SHELL

Found only on White Carnival, this Dugan pattern is rather scarce. The shapes are oval bowls and matching candlesticks. The glass is quite heavy and the luster very rich.

HEAVY WEB

Found primarily on large, thick bowls in peach opalescent, Heavy Web is very interesting Dugan pattern. It has been found with two distinct exterior patterns - a beautifully realistic grape and leaf design covering most of the surface and an equally attractive morning glory pattern. I've seen various shapes including round, ruffled, square and elongated ones. A vivid purple or green bowl in this pattern would certainly be a treasure.

Heavy Hobnail

Heavy Iris

Heavy Pineapple

Heavy Prisms

Heavy Shell

Heavy Web

HERON

Like the Fisherman Mug shown elsewhere in this book, the Dugan attribution is sheer speculation and has been arrived at only by the process of elimination. They simply do not look like products of any of the other known companies that made sizeable amounts of iridized glass. Known only in amethyst, and a very rare marigold, these mugs are much harder to find and must be considered rare. The pattern is on one side of the mug only.

HOBNAIL

While plentiful in many other types of glass, Hobnail is quite a rare item in Carnival and one of real beauty. The very pattern seems perfectly suited for iridescence. The base carries a many rayed design, and all the pieces I've seen are top-notch. The pitchers and tumblers are very rare and extremely hard to locate but even the rose bowl is a prize and the Lady's spittoon is a little darling. Hobnail was made by Millersburg.

HOBNAIL VARIENT

This rare and exciting Millersburg pattern is quite different from the regular Hobnail made by the same company, in that it has 11 rows of dots with 18 in each row around. The top row has only nine hobs however. I suspect this was a copycat item from Fenton's Heavy Hobnail, but it is definitely Millersburg since mold drawings from there exist. Shapes known are vases, rosebowls and a jardinere. Colors reported are marigold, amethyst and green.

HOBNAIL SODA GOLD

While most spittoons found in Carnival glass are of a daintier size, Imperial's Hobnail Soda Gold spittoon is a larger, more practical size. It measures 7″ across the top and stands 5″ high. I've seen examples in marigold and green as well as a peculiar dark shade of amber. Many of these have a great deal of wear on the bottom indicating they were actually used!

HOBSTAR

Apparently this was one of the early near-cut patterns from Imperial. I'd guess it experienced great popularity from the first for it was carried over from crystal to Carnival glass in many shapes, including berry sets, cookie jars, table sets, bride's baskets and a very rare pickle caster in an ornate holder. Marigold is the common color with purple and green quite scarce.

HOBSTAR AND ARCHES

Here is another well-done geometric design from the Imperial Company. Found mostly in bowls, a two piece fruit bowl is available, as shown. Please note the base is the same as that of the Long Hobstar set. Both are correct, and it was unusual for a company to get double mileage where possible. Colors are marigold, green, amethyst and smoke.

HOBSTAR AND CUT TRIANGLES

This very unusual pattern is typically English in design, with strong contrast between geometrically patterned areas against very plain areas. Rose Presznick lists bowls, plates and a rosebowl in this pattern in both green and amethyst, but the only shapes I've seen are bowls, rosebowls and compotes in marigold or amethyst.

Hobnail Variant

102

Heron

Hobnail

Hobnail Soda Gold

Hobstar

Hobstar and Arches

Hobstar and Cut Triangles

HOBSTAR AND FEATHER

If one word could be summoned to describe this Millersburg pattern, that word would be "massive." The glass is thick, the near-cut design deeply cut and impressive. Whether it is a punch bowl, a compote, a giant rosebowl or a pulled vase whimsey, the Hobstar and Feather pattern is not likely to be confused with any other. The usual colors of marigold, green and amethyst are to be found and always in a fine radium finish.

HOBSTAR AND FILE

What a pleasure it is to be able to show this very rare water pitcher (the only one known). Besides the pitcher, two tumblers have been reported. The coloring is a good marigold, and the mould work excellant. It is probably Imperial, but I have no confirmation at this time.

HOBSTAR AND FRUIT

This Westmoreland pattern is known on small and large bowls and a rare 10½″ plate. The bowls are found in peach opalescent mostly, but the small bowl is known in aqua opalescent, and the plate has been found in ice blue.

HOBSTAR BAND

This scarce Imperial pattern is found only on handled celery vases and water sets of two varieties. The usual pitcher is flat based, but as you can see a quite rare pedestal footed variant is known. The only color reported is a good rich marigold.

HOBSTAR FLOWER

This beautiful little Northwood compote is seldom seen and usually comes as a surprise to most collectors. I've heard it called "Octagon" or "Fashion" at one time or another, and most people say they've never seen it before. It is a rather hard to find item. It is known in marigold, but is mostly found in amethyst.

HOBSTAR PANELS

Apparently the English glassmakers like the creamer shape, for they certainly made their share of them. Here is a well-conceived geometric design with hobstars, sunbursts and panels integrated into a very nice whole. The only color I've seen is the deep marigold shown, but certainly there may be others.

HOBSTAR REVERSED

Shown is what was called a "sideboard set" in the advertising by Davisons of Gateshead. It consists of a flower frog and holder that is footed and two side vases which were also used as spooners. Also known is a covered butterdish. The colors listed are marigold, amethyst and blue, but not all colors are found in all shapes.

Hobstar and Feather

Hobstar and Fruit

Hobstar Band

Hobstar Flower

Hobstar Panels　　　　　**Hobstar Reversed**

HOBSTAR WHIRL (WHIRLIGIG)

While I can't be certain who made this very nice compote, I wouldn't rule out Dugan or Northwood. The design is simple but effective, and the luster very good. The coloring is cobalt blue.

HOLLY

Holly is one of the more common Fenton patterns being available in bowls, compotes, goblets, hat shapes and plates. The design is a sound one and tends to look good, especially on the larger bowl and plate shapes. Colors are marigold, green, amethyst, fiery amethyst, blue, aqua opal, white vaseline, ice blue and red. Shown is a beautiful marigold opalescent.

HOLLY AND BERRY

This Dugan pattern, found mostly in rather deep bowls and nappies (one-handled bon-bons) as well as an occasional sauce boat, is so similar to the Millersburg Holly pattern, most people simply accept it as a product of that company. The one distinguishing difference is the leaf and berry medallion in the center of the Holly and Berry pattern while the Millersburg design has no such center motif. Holly and Berry is found in purple, green, marigold, blue and most often peach opalescent. A large piece of this pattern was discovered in the Dugan diggings.

HOLLY SPRIG (or WHIRL)

I have combined these two Millersburg patterns under one title because, frankly, I can distinguish no discernible difference in them. Either can be found with or without a wide panel or the near cut wreath pattern. The holly leaves and berries do vary somewhat from shape to shape but certainly not enough to warrant separate titles. At any rate, it is a simple, well-executed pattern, especially nice on a one-handled nappy. The colors are usually green, marigold and a fine amethyst.

HOLLY WREATH VARIANT (MILLERSBURG)

Besides the Grape Wreath variants, Millersburg's Holly patterns were often given the three same center patterns of feathers, stylized clovers and multi-ringed stars. Here is a very pretty example of the feather center on a bowl with a candy-ribbon edge. All of these are found on 7"-8" bowls in the usual Millersburg colors.

HONEYBEE POT

First drawn by Rose Presznick, this cute novelty item is first rate. The coloring is very yellow and really suits the purpose in every way with even a slot for a spoon to dip the honey.

HONEYCOMB AND CLOVER

While this Fenton pattern is best known as the exterior design of Feathered Serpent pieces, it is also used as the primary pattern for bon-bons and the scarce compote. Colors I've heard about include marigold, green, blue, amethyst, amber and white but others may exist!

Honeybee Pot   **Holly Wreath Variant
(Millersburg)**

Hobstar Whirl

Holiday

Holly

Holly and Berry

Holly Sprig (or Whirl)

Honeycomb and Clover

HONEYCOMB AND HOBSTAR

This very rare vase is from the Millersburg Company and has never been out of the Ohio area. As you can see, it is a very rich blue with heavy even luster. The base design is the same as the Hobstar and Feather rosebowl. The vase stands 8¼″ tall. This example was found years ago on a shelf in a defunct Millersburg business and has remained in its present home for many years. Another blue and one amethyst are reported.

HONEYCOMB ROSEBOWL

The latest shards from the Dugan digs have turned up two large pieces of this pattern, so Dugan was the maker. The Honeycomb Rosebowl is a rare item, found in both marigold and peach opalescent.

HORN OF PLENTY

What can I say about this bottle that isn't obvious from the photo? It isn't rare or even good Carnival, but it certainly has a place in the history of our glass.

HORSES' HEADS

Sometimes called Horse Medallion, this well known Fenton pattern can be found in flat or footed bowls, a scarce plate shape and the rare rose bowl. The edges often are varied in ruffling and can resemble a jack-in-the-pulpit shape. Colors are marigold, blue, green, white, vaseline, aqua and red.

HORSESHOE SHOT GLASS

If it weren't for the pretty horseshoe design in the bottom of this shot glass, it would be just another piece of glass. But with the design, it is very collectible, highly sought and not cheap. Marigold is the only color so far reported.

HOT SPRINGS VASE

This very interesting vase is a beauty. It measures 9⅞″ tall and 4½″ wide across the top. The coloring is a pale amber and the iridescence is quite good.

It is lettered:

"To Lena from Uncle
Hot Springs, Arkansas
Superior Bath House
May 20, 1903"

Who says Carnival glass was first made in 1907?

IDYLL (FENTON)

While I apologize for the poor quality of the picture, I have only praise for this very rare vase. It is one of only two ever reported and is a design jewel. The coloring is amethyst, and it stands 7″ tall. The pattern of water-lillies and butterflies is just right.

ILLINOIS DAISY

How strange the name of this pattern sounds on a British pattern, but Illinois Daisy was a product of Davisons of Gateshead. Shapes known are the familiar covered jar and an 8″ bowl. The only color I've heard about is marigold, often very weak, but perhaps time will turn up another color.

ILLUSION

It is rather difficult to describe this seldom discussed Fenton pattern. It is found on bowls occasionally, but mainly on bon-bons and is a combination of flowers, leaves and odd geometric shadow-like blotches. Colors seen are marigold and blue, but I certainly would rule out green amethyst. A red Illusion bon-bon would be a real treasure, but so far I haven't heard of one.

Idyll (Fenton)

Honeycomb and Hobstar

Honeycomb Rosebowl

Horseshoe Shot Glass

Horses' Heads

Horn of Plenty

Hot Springs Vase

Illinois Daisy

Illusion

IMPERIAL BASKET

This Imperial handled basket is identical in size and shape to the Daisy basket and as you can see, the handle patterns are the same. The coloring is unusual in that it is mostly smoke Carnival with just a touch of marigold around the top.

IMPERIAL JEWELS CANDLE HOLDER

These beautiful Imperial Jewels Candlesticks are 7¼″ tall. As you can see, they have a bold red iridized finish, and there is no stretch effect. Some are makred with the "Iron Cross" mark, but these are not.

IMPERIAL PAPERWEIGHT

This very rare advertising paperweight was shown in my recent book on Carnival glass rarities for very few of these are known. The paperweight is roughly rectangular, 5½″ long, 3⅛″ wide and 1″ thick. A depressed oval is in the center of the weight and it is inscribed: "Imperial Glass Company, Bellaire, Ohio, USA," "Imperial Art Glass," "Nucut," "NuArt," and "IM | PE." These are all trademarks of the company, of course. The glass is a fine amethyst
RI | AL
with good, rich lustre.

INCA VASE

Like its sister design, the Sea Gulls vase, this is a foreign pattern also. It's probably Scandinavian. The feeling is Art Deco and very well done. The only color reported is a rich marigold.

INDIANA STATEHOUSE

Besides the two versions of the Soldiers and Sailors plates, Fenton also made this very rare plate shown in blue. The size is identical to the other two and the exterior carries the same Berry and Leaf Circle design. This was made in marigold also.

INTAGLIO DAISY

Again, the English have designed a neat, useful near-cut pattern. The bowl stands 4″ tall and has a 7½″ width. The design is all intaglio, and the only color I've seen is marigold. Sowerby is the maker.

Imperial Basket

Imperial Candle Holder

Imperial Paperweight

Inca Vase

Indiana Statehouse

Intaglio Daisy

INTERIOR FLUTE

Here's another one of the many flute patterns so popular in their day. There was probably a matching sugar, and I haven't seen any other colors but they probably exist.

INTERIOR RAYS

The three-piece table set, consisting of covered butterdish, covered sugar and covered jam jar came from Australia. Whether it was made there, I can't say, but I'd guess England as its original home.

INTERIOR RIB (IMPERIAL)

This very classy 7½″ vase is tissue paper thin, and the only design is the inside ribbing that runs the length of the glass. The color is a strong smoke with high luster, and I've seen only two of these over the years.

INTERIOR SWIRL AND WIDE PANEL

Despite its long name, this squat pitcher is a real cute one with good coloring and lots of charcter. Other colors and shapes may exist, but I haven't seen them, and I don't know who the maker is.

INVERTED COIN DOT

The tumbler shown is part of a scarce water set made by the Fenton company, and to the best of my knowledge is not found in other shapes. As you can see, the pattern is all interior. Colors known are marigold, amethyst and green, but blue may exist.

INVERTED FEATHER

This is probably the best known of all Cambridge Carnival glass patterns and is found in a variety of shapes including a cracker jar, table set, water set, compote, sherbet, wine, milk pitcher and punch set. All shapes are rare except the cracker jar, and colors known are marigold, green and amethyst.

INVERTED STRAWBERRY

Like its cousin, Inverted Thistle, this beautiful Cambridge pattern is all intaglio and can be found on several shapes including berry sets, water sets, candlesticks, large compotes, sherbets, milk pitchers, creamers, spooners, a stemmed celery, powder jars and a ladies spittoon. All shapes are rare and colors known are marigold, green, amethyst and blue.

INVERTED THISTLE

Cambridge was responsible for very original patterns and superior workmanship and here is a prime example. Known in water sets, a spittoon, a covered box, a pickle dish and a breakfast set, this is an intaglio pattern. Colors are marigold, amethyst, green and a rare blue.

IRIS

Along with the plain Buttermilk Goblet, this pattern found in both compotes and goblets, has created a good deal of controversy, for some have felt it was a Millersburg product. However, I'm convinced it is Fenton. Colors seen are marigold, green, amethyst and a very rare white.

IRIS AND HERRINGBONE

Made late in Carnival history, this Jeanette pattern can be found in a host of shapes, all useful. Its coloring runs from good to awful, and many pieces are found in crystal also.

Iris and Herringbone   112   **Interior Swirl and Wide Panel**

Interior Rays

Inverted Coin Dot

Interior Flute

Inverted Feather

Inverted Strawberry

Inverted Thistle (Late)

Interior Rib

Iris

ISAAC BENESCH BOWL

This cute 6¼" advertising bowl is quite easily identified because of its distinct design. It bears the labeling "The Great House of Isaac Benesch and Sons, Wilksbarre, Pa., Baltimore, Md., Annapolis, MD." The center theme is bracketed by sprigs of daisy-like blossoms and leaves. The exterior carries the familiar wide panel design and a rayed base. The predominant color is amethyst.

IVY

This cute little souvenir wine has the same stem and base design as Fenton's small Orange Tree compote so we are sure it came from that factory. It is found in both the wine and claret size with various advertisements. Marigold is the only color I've seen but certainly others may have been made.

JACK-IN-THE-PULPIT

While both Dugan and Fenton made Jack-in-the-Pulpit vases, the one shown is a Northwood pattern and is so marked. It stands 8¼" tall and has an exterior ribbing. Colors known are marigold, purple, green, aqua opalescent and white but others may exist.

JACK-IN-THE-PULPIT (DUGAN)

Besides the Northwood version of this vase, Dugan had a try at it too and here is their version. It's a bit plainer and isn't nearly as pretty without the footing but it does come in several colors and adds a pleasant touch of color and artistry.

JACKMAN WHISKEY

Much like its cousin, the Golden Wedding bottle, this was designed to hold whiskey for commercial sale. It is scarcer than the former and generally has better iridescence. The maker is unknown.

JACOB'S LADDER VARIANT (U.S. GLASS)

Besides the Jacob's Ladder perfume, I've heard of this rose bowl shape in the variant and nothing else. Just why more shapes haven't surfaced, I don't know, for the pattern is interesting and well-done. The only color is a good marigold.

JELLY JAR

For years I found the lids to these Imperial Jelly Jars in shops and thought they were late Carnival glass "coasters," but a few years back, I saw the two parts put together and was really quite surprised at what I saw. The jar itself is 3" wide and 2¾" tall and of deep, well iridized marigold. All the pattern is interior so that when the jar was upended onto the lid, a design was formed in the jelly. The lid itself also carries an interior design of spokes and an exterior one of a many-rayed star. Again, here is a true rarity, well within any collector's range.

JEWELED HEART

Carried over from the pressed glass era, Jeweled Heart is, of course, the famous exterior pattern of the Farmyard bowl. However, Dugan used it as a primary pattern on very scarce water sets when the pitcher is footed - an uncommon shape for water pitchers in Carnival glass. I have seen Jeweled Heart in purple, peach and marigold but other colors may exist. If so, they would be considered ultra-rare. A tumbler is reported in white, but I haven't seen it.

JEWELS

This was the name given to a line of unpatterned iridized glass make by the Imperial Company at the same time they were making their wonderful Carnival. Whether you consider it Carnival glass is your business, but I do, so I'm showing it here. It was made in a multitude of shapes and most Imperial colors.

Jack-in-the-Pulpit (Dugan)

Jacob's Ladder Variant (U.S. Glass)

Isaac Benesch Bowl

Jack-in-the-Pulpit

Jackman Whiskey

Ivy (Wine)

Jelly Jar

Jeweled Heart

Jewels

115

JOCKEY CLUB
Although very much akin to the Good Luck pattern, Northwood's Jockey Club iss certainly a separate pattern and a quick once-over will establish this fact. The floral arrangements are entirely different, even the horse-shoe and riding crop are not the same. Jockey Club is found on trade-marked bowls which carry the Northwood Basketweave as an exterior pattern. The ones I'm familiar with have been on a good amethyst glass, well iridized.

KANGAROO
This beautiful Australian pattern typifies the quality of the Crystal Glass Factory. Known in large and small bowls, in marigold and purple, Kangaroo has the Wild Fern pattern as its exterior. There is a variant.

KEYHOLE (DUGAN)
Used as the exterior pattern on Raindrop bowls, this Dugan secondary pattern is much more interesting than the one it compliments. Colors are marigold, amethyst and peach opalescent.

KEYSTONE COLONIAL (WESTMORELAND)
At least three of these have been reported, all with the keystone trademark containing a "W." They stand 6¼" tall and are very much like the Chippendale pattern compotes credited to Jefferson Glass. The only color I've seen is a very dark purple.

KINGFISHER
Like many of the other "bird patterns" from down under, this nice Australian bowl has both the animal and flora shown. Kingfisher has a stippled aura, a registration number, and comes in large and small bowls.

KINGFISHER VARIANT
The primary difference between this and the regular Australian Kingfisher pattern is the addition of a wreath of wattle. Both marigold and purple are found.

KING'S CROWN (U.S. GLASS)
In crystal and ruby flashed glass, this pattern can be found in many shapes, but this is the only piece in Carnival glass I've ever heard about. It is a dainty wine goblet in good marigold and very, very rare indeed.

KITTEN PAPERWEIGHT
This slight bit of glass is a rare miniature heretofore unreported in any of the pattern books on Carnival glass. Its coloring, as you can see, is a good even marigold, and the iridization is well applied. In size, it is much like the 3″ long Bulldog paperweight. The Kitten paperweight is truly a rare little item.

KITTENS
For many years, this Fenton pattern has been a favorite of collectors and the Kittens pieces rise steadily in price and popularity. This is a child's pattern and is known in bowls, cup and saucer, banana bowl, spooner, plate, vase and a very rare spittoon whimsey. Colors are marigold, vaseline and cobalt blue.

King's Crown (U.S. Glass)

Keystone Colonial (Westmoreland)

Jockey Club

Kangaroo

Kingfisher

Kingfisher Vt

Kitten Paperweight

Kittens

Keyhole (Dugan)

KIWI

This very odd bird is a native of New Zealand. This Australian bowl shows two of them, with a mountain range in the background and a border of fine fern branches. Colors are a fine purple and marigold.

KNOTTED BEADS

In many ways, this is a combination of the April Showers vase pattern and the Diamond and Rib vase pattern for the tiny bead grouping are gathered into pulled ovals. I know of examples of Knotted Beads in marigold, blue, green, white and vaseline, and sizes range from 4″ to 12″ in height. A Fenton product.

KOOKABURRA

Similar to the Kingfisher pattern, the Australian Kookaburra has an upper edging of Flannel Flower, wattle and two large groups of Waratah flowers flanking a Flannel Flower blossom.

KOOKABURA VARIANT

In this Australian variant, the obvious differences are the fine large Waratah flowers around the stippled circle. And, of course, the edging is a bullet rim pattern.

LBJ HAT

This late Carnival ashtray has been called this for the last few years. It has a diameter of 6¼″ and stands 3″ tall. While not in the class of a Cleveland Memorial Ashtray, it is an attractive specimen of iridized glass.

LACY DEWDROP

Lacy Dewdrop appears in iridized glass in one way only - the pearl Carnival shown. Shapes reported are pitchers, tumblers, covered compotes, covered bowls and banana bowls. Westmoreland is the possible maker.

LATE WATERLILY

For one of the later patterns in Carnival glass, this certainly is a good one. The coloring is superior, the shape symetrical, and the design of cattails and waterlilies attractive.

Late Waterlily

Kiwi

Knotted Beads

Kookaburra

Kookabura Vt.

LBJ Hat

Lacy Dewdrop

LATTICE AND DAISY

Most often seen on marigold water sets, Dugan's Lattice and Daisy was also made on very scarce berry sets. The other colors known are cobalt blue and white, but I certainly would not rule out green or amethyst, especially on the water sets.

LATTICE AND GRAPE

If you examine the shape of this Fenton water set, you'll find it is almost identical to that of the Grapevine Lattice water set, but Lattice and Grape is distinctive in its own right. The mold work is very good and the design appealing. Available in a rare spittoon whimsey pulled from a tumbler in addition to water sets, Lattice and Grape is found in marigold, cobalt blue, green, amethyst, peach opalescent and white.

LAUREL AND GRAPE

I know very little about this previously unreported pattern except that it is a vase shape and stands 7″ tall. The design, a cluster of grapes inside a laurel wreath is a nice one and reminds me of the English Grape and Cherry pattern. Marigold is the only reported color.

LEA

Found in a handled pickle dish, a footed creamer, and a footed bowl that can be in various shapes, Lea and the Lea variants are patterns produced by the Sowerby company. Most examples are marigold, but I have heard of an amethyst creamer.

LEAF AND BEADS

Here is another very well known Northwood pattern found not only in Carnival glass, but clear and opalescent glass as well. Available on bowls as well as rose bowls, the twig feet are used by more than one Carnival glass maker. However, the trade mark is usually present. Leaf and Beads is found in a wide range of colors including marigold, green, purple, ice green, ice blue and white.

LEAF AND BEADS VARIANT

Here is the variant bowl on a dome base and as you can see, the design is not so strong as the regular Leaf and Beads. These seem to be found mostly in green, as shown, but marigold and amethyst are known. It is marked Northwood. The shape is considered a nut bowl by many collectors.

LEAF AND LITTLE FLOWERS

This little Millersburg cutie is rather unique, not only in size but also in design. The four free-floating blooms are similar to those on the Little Stars design, but the four large prickly-edged leaves with a center cross blossom is unique. It seems cactus-like. Just 3″ tall, the Leaf and Little Flowers compote, has an octagon shaped base and has been seen in amethyst, green and rarely marigold.

LEAF CHAIN

Very close to Cherry Chain in design, Fenton's Leaf Chain is more commonly found, indicating it was made in larger amounts. Known in bowls, plates and bon-bons. Leaf Chain was made in a wide variety of colors including marigold, cobalt blue, green, amethyst, white, vaseline, lavender, smoke, aqua and red. The mold work is quite good and the finish above average. Shown in a rare marigold opalescent.

Leaf and Beads Variant

120

Laurel and Grape

Lattice and Daisy

Lattice and Grape

Leaf and Beads

Lea

Leaf and Little Flowers

Leaf Chain

LEAF COLUMN

While not a spectacular pattern, here is a Northwood vase that takes on new importance on second glance. It is a well-balanced all-over pattern that does the job nicely. The iridescence, especially on the dark colors, is quite nice. The shape is attractive and the vase is, of course, a very useful item. Certainly any collection of Carnival glass would benefit by adding one of these.

LEAF RAYS

Found mostly on a one-handled, spade shaped nappy, this Dugan pattern was also made in the ruffled version shown. Colors are marigold, peach opalescent, amethyst, green, blue, white and clear.

LEAF SWIRL

Here is a much overlooked pattern and that certainly is a shame because it is a beautiful, well-executed one. This compote is almost 5″ tall and has three mold marks. It is usually found on a very deep shade of purple, but we are delighted to show you this teal color so very rare. Amber and marigold are also known. A Westmoreland product.

LEAF SWIRL AND FLOWER

What a beautifully graceful vase this is. It appears to be a Fenton product, stands 8″ tall and has a trail of etched leaves and flowers around the body. I'd guess it was made in marigold and other pastels too, but can't be sure.

LEAF TIERS

For some reason, this pattern is difficult to locate, so apparently it wasn't made in large quantities although it was made in useable shapes, including berry sets, table sets and water sets. The twig feet were used by both Fenton and Northwood to some degree, and while Leaf Tiers is mostly seen in marigold, very scarce water sets in purple, green and blue are known. A Fenton product.

LILY OF THE VALLEY

Personally, I feel this is the very best of all Fenton water sets, and the price this rare pattern commands bears me out. Aside from being beautiful, Lily of the Valley is an imaginative pattern. Found only in cobalt blue and marigold, Lily of the Valley would have made a beautiful table set pattern.

Leaf Column

Leaf Rays

Leaf Swirl

Leaf Swirl and Flower

Leaf Tiers

Lily of the Valley

LINED LATTICE

Most often seen in a vase shape with odd feet-like projections, the same design is used on a shade frequently associated with the Princess lamp base. The vase, we know, was made by Dugan and can be found in marigold, amethyst, blue, green, peach opalescent and white.

LION

Someone at the Fenton factory had to be an animal lover for more animal patterns were born there than at any other Carnival glass factory in America. The Lion pattern is a nice one, rather scarce and available in bowls and plates. The colors are marigold and blue in the bowls, but I've seen only marigold in the rare plates.

LITTLE BARREL

I have no proof that this is an Imperial design; however, the lustre, mold work and the color of helios green, marigold, amber and smoke all suggest the Little Barrel is an Imperial product. They are rumored to have held a sample of some liquid and examples have been found with paper labels on the exterior suggesting a giveaway item. Nonetheless, they are hard to find, very collectible and much loved.

LITTLE BEADS

Made by the Dugan Company, this odd little pattern is seen mostly on peach opal, but the example shown has a pink base glass. It measures 2″ tall, 5½″ across and has a 2½″ base.

LITTLE DAISIES

Apparently Fenton made very small amounts of this pattern for few examples are to be found. Marigold is the only color reported and the only bowl shape found. The exterior is plain.

LITTLE FISHES

A close comparison with the Coral pattern will reveal many similarities to this pattern. Little Fishes can be found in large or small bowls, both flat based and footed, and in rare plates that measure about 9″. Colors are marigold, blue, green, amethyst, aqua, vaseline, amber, ice green and white, which is rather rare.

Lined Lattice

Lion

Little Barrel

Little Beads

Little Daisies

Little Fishes

LITTLE FLOWERS

Here's another pattern once felt to be Millersburg but now known to be a Fenton product. Little Flowers is found in berry sets and two sizes of rare plates, in marigold, green, blue amethyst, amber, aqua, vaseline and red.

LITTLE STARS

I've found this Millersburg pattern a bit difficult to locate and don't believe many of these bowls are around. The amethyst ones are especially nice, but green and marigold exist. Also a larger size is known as is the plate shape in green. Shown is a rare blue bowl.

LOGANBERRY

Despite the reproduction of this impressive vase in the 1960s, Imperial's Loganberry has remained one of the collector's favorites. The vase is 10″ tall and has a base diameter of 3¾″. There are four mold marks. The colors found are green, marigold, amber, smoke and purple with the latter hardest to find. Of course, the quality of design and the beautiful lustre make this a real treasure.

LONG HOBSTAR

Imperial was famous for near-cut designs, and Long Hobstar is a prime example of their skill. Shown is a very rare punch bowl and base (no cups known), but Long Hobstar can also be found in bowls, and a beautiful Bride's Basket. The colors are marigold, smoke, green and occasionally purple.

LONG THUMBPRINT

Found in bowls, compotes, creamers, sugars and vases, this Dugan pattern has little going for it design-wise, but sometimes is quite nice when the coloring is as good as on the vase shown. Colors are mostly marigold, but amethyst, blue and green are occasionally found and I've seen the breakfast pieces in a smoky marigold, and the vase in peach opalescent.

LOTUS AND GRAPE

Please note the similarities between this pattern and Fenton's Water Lily and Two Flowers. All have a feeling of the small ponds once so much a part of back yard garden displays. Lotus and Grape is found on bon-bons, flat or footed bowls, and rare plates in colors of marigold, green, blue, amethyst, white and red.

LOTUS LAND

What a privilege to show this rare, rare bon-bon, generous in size (8¼″ across) and rich in design. From its stippled center flower to the whimsical outer flowers, the pattern is one you won't soon forget. Amethyst is the only reported color on the few examples.

Lotus Land

Little Flowers

Little Stars

Loganberry

Long Hobstar

Long Thumbprint

Lotus and Grape

LOUISA

Louisa is a very pretty, well designed floral pattern that seems perfectly suited for the rose bowl shape shown. Also known on footed candy dishes and a rare footed plate (all from the same mold), Louisa is found in marigold, green, blue, amethyst, and the rare deep amber called "horehound." This is by Westmoreland.

LOVELY

Northwood's Lovely is a seldom seen interior pattern found on footed bowls with Leaf and Beads as an exterior pattern. While we can't be certain, it is possible this motif was added at the Dugan factory since shards of Leaf and Beads were found there. The colors seen thus far are marigold and purple with very good iridescence.

LUSTRE AND CLEAR

Most often seen in footed creamer and open sugar, I've seen Lustre and Clear on a beautiful Clambroth rosebowl (marked with the old "Ironcross" mark), bowls of several sizes, a celery tray, water sets, a compote and a fan vase. Originally called Pillar and Flute (#682), this Imperial pattern was made in many, many shapes in crystal. The usual colors are marigold or smoke with an occasional green or purple piece appearing.

LUSTRE FLUTE

Again we have a very familiar pattern to most collectors, but one that is not really too distinguished. I suppose not every pattern should be expected to be spectacular. The shape I've seen most often is the hat shape in both green and marigold, but punch sets, berry sets, breakfast sets, bon-bons, nappies and compotes do exist in marigold, green and purple. The base is many-rayed and usually the Northwood trademark is present.

LUSTRE ROSE

Aside from Imperial's Grape or Pansy patterns, this is probably their biggest seller in the early years and was made in berry sets, table sets, water sets, plates, fruit bowls and a beautiful fernery in colors of marigold, green, purple, cobalt, amber, smoke and clambroth. Reproduction has devalued this beautiful pattern, but the old pieces are still outstanding examples of glass making, with superb craftsmanship and color.

MADAY AND CO.

This quite rare advertising bowl is found as the exterior of Fenton's Wild Blackberry 8½″ bowl. The only color known to date is amethyst, while the normal bowls are found in green and marigold primarily. The advertising reads: "H. Maday and Co. 1910."

MAGPIE

The Magpie is a different bird altogether and the one shown on this Australian bowl is probably a New Zealand Parson bird. The flowers are typical Flannel Flowers and wattle.

Maday and Co.

Louisa

Lovely

Lustre and Clear

Lustre Flute

Lustre Rose

Magpie

MALAGA

Malaga is a rather difficult pattern to find, indicating production must have been small on this Dugan design. What a pity for the all-over grape pattern is a good one with imaginative detail throughout. Found only on large bowls and plates, I've heard of marigold, amber and purple only, but green is a strong possibility.

MALLARD DUCK

I certainly wish I knew more about this rare item, but it's the only true Carnival one I've seen. I believe these were made by Tiffin (mostly in milk glass), and I once saw an example with applied ruby lustre. However, I can say with assurance the one shown is old, has been in one of the country's major collections for years and is a prized rarity of the owner. The coloring is a beautiful clambroth with fiery blue and pink highlights.

MANY FRUITS

This is a truly lovely fruit pattern, something that any company would be proud to claim. The mold work is heavy and distinct, the design is interesting and quite realistic and the coloration flawless. I personally prefer the ruffled base, but that is a small matter. This Dugan pattern would have made a beautiful water set. The colors are marigold, blue, white, purple and green.

MANY STARS

Which came first - the chicken or the egg? Or in this case, the Many Stars or the Bernheimer bowl? For they are exactly the same except for the center design where in the former a large star replaces the advertising. These bowls are generous in size and can be found in amethyst, green, marigold and blue. The green is often a light, airy shade just a bit darker than an ice green and is very attractive when found with a gold iridescence. Millersburg manufactured this pattern.

MAPLE LEAF

Maple Leaf is a carry-over pattern from the custard glass line, but in Carnival glass is limited to stemmed berry sets, table sets and water sets. I examined shards of this patern from the Dugan dump site, so items in Carnival glass were obviously turned out at that factory. The background is the same Soda Gold pattern as that found on the exterior of Garden Path bowls and plates. Maple Leaf was made in marigold, purple, cobalt blue and green.

MARILYN

This water set pattern is probably one of the most unusual and outstanding in the field of Carnival glass. First look at the pitcher's shape. Notice the unusual upper edging, so different than those of other companies. Then there is the drooping pouring lip so favored by the Millersburg company. The finish is, of course, the fine radium look and the glass is heavy. All in all, a real prize for any collector.

MARY ANN

I don't believe I've heard of another one of these loving cups in collections I'm familiar with, and yet I've always known these existed. As you can see, they are much different from the vase shape, having three handles and no scalloping around the top edge or base. Of course, it is quite rare, and it is a real pleasure to show it here. The Mary Ann vase is Dugan.

MASSACHUSETTS (U.S. GLASS)

While the vase shape shown is the only shape I've heard about in this very attractive pattern, I'd bet it was made in a creamer and sugar as well. It is found only in marigold and brings a good price when sold for it a scarce and desirable item.

Mary Ann

Malaga

Mallard Duck

Many Fruits

·Many Stars

Maple Leaf

Massachusetts

Marilyn

MAY BASKET

This beautiful basket is called Diamond and Fleur de lis by Mrs. Presznick. It was made by Davisons of Gateshead and has a diameter of 7½″ and is 6″ tall. Can you imagine how difficult it was to remove this beautiful novelty from the mold? May Basket was made in marigold and has been reported in smoke.

MAYAN

Mayan is quite unique pattern; once seen, it is easily identified. Its six feather-like plumes stand out proundly from the raised, beaded button-center. Of course, the beaded border is a Millersburg favorite that appears on the Daisy Square pedestal rose-bowl as well as the Olympic compote.

MAYFLOWER (MILLERSBURG)

Found with the rare Millersburg Grape Leaves bowl, Mayflower is a series of flower-like designs, separated by eight diamond and near-cut sections. Held to the light, the effect is a real surprise through the Grape design. Colors are marigold, green, amethyst and vaseline and every one is rare.

MEANDER (NORTHWOOD)

Here's the exterior of the gorgeous Three Fruits Medallion bowl shown elsewhere, and as you can see, the glass is truly black amethyst and has no iridizing on the exterior. The pattern of Meander, however, is a good design and very complimentary.

MELON RIB

Another pattern credited to Imperial, Melon Rib can be found on water sets, candy jars, salt and pepper shakers and a covered powder jar, all in marigold. As you can see, the pitcher is tall and stately and very pretty.

MEMPHIS

While an interesting geometrical pattern, Northwood's Memphis has never been one of my favorites - possibly because of its limited shapes. I can imagine how much my interest would increase if a water set were to appear! I have seen an enormous banquet punch set in crystal, but the size was not made in Carnival glass. The shapes are a berry set, punch set, fruit bowl on separate stand, and a compote. The colors found are both vivid and pastel.

MIKADO

Called giant compotes, these beautiful 8½″ tall fruit stands have two outstanding patterns - cherries on the exterior and the beautiful Mikado on the inside of the bowl. This design consists of a center Medallion of stippled rays around which are three large chrysanthemums and three oriental scroll devices. The colors are marigold, blue, a rare green and a very rare red. Mikado was made by Fenton.

MILADY

Again, we show one of the better water sets by the Fenton Company. The pitcher is a tankard size, and the design is panelled with very artistic blossoms and stems with graceful leaves. Colors most seen are marigold and blue, but scarce green and a rare amethyst do exist as shown.

Mayflower (Millersburg)

Meander (Northwood)

132

Melon Rib

May Basket

Mayan

Memphis

Mikado

Milady

MINIATURE BLACKBERRY COMPOTE

This little Fenton cutie is most often seen on blue or marigold and is quite scarce in either color. The white one shown is very rare. Standing only 2½" high with a bowl diameter of 4⅛", this miniature or jelly compote would be a treasure in any collection and certainly would highlight a compote grouping.

MINIATURE HOBNAIL CORDIAL SET

What a nice little set this is! Probably from Europe, it is the only one I've heard about. The decanter stands 8" tall to the top of its stopper and needless to say, the set is quite a rare item.

MIRRORED LOTUS

Besides a rare white rosebowl, Fenton's Mirrored Lotus is most seen in a 7" ruffled bowl in blue, green, marigold or white. A bon bon shape and a plate shape are also known.

MITERED DIAMONDS AND PLEATS

This British pattern is most often seen as shown, a 4½" handled sauce dish, but I've seen 8½" bowls and Mrs. Presznick reports a tray in 10" size as well. The coloring is top notch marigold, but a smoky blue shade has been reported.

MITERED OVALS

Although this beautiful vase has long been considered an Imperial pattern, there's no doubt it is a Millersburg product. It is a rare item seldom found for sale. The colors seen are amethyst, green and very rarely marigold. In size, it is outstanding, being some 10½" tall. The mold work is superior.

MODERNE

I've named this cute cup and saucer the very first name that entered my head, but it seems to fit. I'd guess it is fairly late Carnival, but it still has good coloring and a nice lustre.

MOONPRINT

Here is one of the pretties of all English Carnival patterns. The shapes are a banana bowl, covered jar, vase, covered butter, covered cheesekeeper, compote, milk pitcher, creamer and bowls that range in size from 8" to 15". Marigold is the basic color with a super finish. I've heard of a peach opalescent covered jar but cannot confirm its existence. I'd guess Sowerby made this pattern.

MORNING GLORY

If there is one water set that stands above all others in sheer beauty, this Millersburg pattern is surely it. Almost 14" tall, the pitcher is stately. The heavily raised morning glory vines around its center and the applied handle has been shaped to resemble a leaf where it joins the pitcher. The matching tumbler is 3¾" tall and has a rayed base. The glass is sparkling clear, the radium finish is excellent and the mold work impressive. Along with the Gay 90's, the Morning Glory water set has to be near the top of anyone's list.

Moderne

134   **Miniature Hobnail Cordial Set**

Miniature Blackberry Compote

Mirrored Lotus

Mitered Diamonds and Pleats

Mitered Ovals

Moonprint

Morning Glory

MORNING GLORY VASE

Several companies made similar vases with the flaring top resembling morning glories, but the one shown happens to come from Imperial and is a whopping 17″ tall. The color is fabulous! I've seen these as small as 8″ and every size between, in several colors including marigold, smoke, green, blue, amethyst, white, ice green, teal and aqua ... even one in a strange pale blue and marigold combination.

MT. GAMBIER MUG

I can't be sure this mug is Australian, but this one comes from there. It is etched "Greetings from Mt. Gambier." The color is a good rich marigold.

MOXIE BOTTLE

I normally avoid the bottle cycle unless they are attractive as this well-designed scarcity. The coloring is obviously a very frosty white with heavy luster, and the design of plain and stippled diamonds is a good one. Moxie was a soft drink that went out of favor in the mid 1920s.

MULTI-FRUITS AND FLOWERS

Grape clusters, leaves, blossoms, cherries, peaches and pears! What an imaginative collection to grace beautiful lustered glass! This fantastic Millersburg pattern is seen mostly on punch sets of medium size, but there is a very scarce water set and a stemmed fruit goblet or compote. The base of the punch set can double as a compote when up-ended and is iridized inside and out.

MY LADY'S POWDER BOX

Here is a favorite with collectors and a good price is always assured when one of these sell. Found only in marigold of a good rich quality, the powder jar stands 5½″ tall and has a base diameter of 3¼″. The figure on the lid is of solid glass. I suspect Davisons is the manufacturer, but have no proof.

MYSTIC

I named this 7″ vase so if anyone knows it by another name, I'd be happy to hear from them. The design of elongated shields separated by a hobstar and file filler is interesting and the very mellow coloring reminds me of some Cambridge products, but I can't be sure just who made it.

NAUTILIS

It is a shame there aren't more shapes of this pattern in Carnival glass because every piece of the custard shapes are a joy. In Carnival we find only the small novelty piece described as a boat shape (actually one large footed berry bowl has been seen in marigold - a very, very rare piece of Carnival glass! It appears with either both ends turned up or one end turned down, and the colors are peach and purple. A Dugan product from old Northwood moulds.

NEAR-CUT

This attractive Northwood pattern is quite similar to the Hobstar Flower shown elsewhere in this book. In addition to the compote and goblet, made from the same mold, there is a very rare water pitcher. I have heard of no tumblers but they may exist. The colors are marigold and purple with the latter most seen. A rare green compote is known also.

Mystic

Mt. Gambier Mug

Moxie Bottle

Multi-Fruits and Flowers

My Lady's Powder Box

Nautilis

Morning Glory

Near-Cut

137

NEAR CUT DECANTER

What a triumph of near cut design this rare Cambridge pattern is! Standing 11″ tall, this beauty is found in a sparkling green, but I wouldn't rule out amethyst or marigold as possibilities. The mold work is some of the best, and the finish is equal to any from the Millersburg plant.

NESTING SWAN

This pattern has become one of the most sought Millersburg bowl patterns, and it is certainly easy to see why. The graceful swan, nesting on a bed of reeds, surrounded by leaves and blossoms and cattails is a very interesting design. The detail is quite good and the color and finish exceptional. The beautiful Diamond and Fan exterior contrasts nicely and echoes the fine workmanship throughout. In addition to the beautiful green, marigold and amethyst, Nesting Swan can be found in a beautiful honey-amber shade and a very rare blue.

NEW ORLEANS CHAMPAGNE

Like the other champagnes, from U.S. Glass, this version is on clear iridized glass with the design areas hand painted. The alligators along the sides are quite unique in Carnival glass and the crowned and bearded man represents Rex, King of the Mardi Gras. I really can't think of anything more fitting for a piece of Carnival glass.

NIGHT STARS

What a rare little beauty this Millersburg pattern is! Found on the bon-bon shape shown in an unusual olive green, marigold and amethyst, it has also been seen in a very rare card tray in amethyst and vaseline and an equally rare spade-shaped nappy in amethyst only. All shapes and colors are rare and desirable so never pass one up.

NIPPON

Certainly Nippon must have been a popular pattern in its heyday, for it is readily found today. The pattern is simple but effective; a central stylized blossom with panels of drapery extending toward the outer edges of the bowl. Found in a wide variety of colors, including marigold, green, blue, purple, ice green, ice blue and white. This Northwood is a nice pattern to own.

NORTHERN STAR

I have some misgivings about this being a Fenton pattern, but since it is listed as such by a noted glass author, I will consider it one. Shown is the 6″ card tray, but Northern Star can also be found on a ruffled mint dish, small bowls and plates, all in marigold. The design is all on the exterior and both outside and inside are iridized.

Near Cut Decanter

Nesting Swan

New Orleans Champagne

Night Stars

Nippon

139

Northern Star

NU-ART CHRYSANTHEMUM

Apparently the popularity of the regular Nu-Art plate prompted this, a sister design of striking beauty. Also 10½″ in diameter, the Chrysanthemum plate has the same Greek key border device. The flowers are very graceful and heavily raised and, of couse, the iridescence is outstanding. I've seen this plate in marigold, smoke, amber, green, clambroth and purple, but other colors may exist. Again, this pattern was reproduced in the 1960s. This was produced by Imperial.

NU-ART (HOMESTEAD)

If you will take a few moments to compare this Imperial pattern with the Double Dutch found elsewhere in this book, you will find very similar designs, probably done by the same artist. The Nu-Art plate, however, is a rarer more important design that sells for many times the amount of a Double Dutch bowl. Found in many colors including marigold, green, purple, smoke, amber, white, ice green and the rare cobalt blue, the Nu-Art plate is sometimes signed. It measures 10½″ across and has been reproduced.

#5

This pattern dates from the early days of the Imperial Company and was first issued in crystal. The shapes known are a celery holder, 6″ tall, and the beautiful dome-footed bowl shown, where the pattern is exterior. The color most encountered is marigold, but as you can see, the bowl is a rich amber.

#4

Made first in crystal, like so many Imperial patterns, this is a rather simple, not too impressive pattern, found on compotes as well as small footed bowls. The colors are usually marigold or smoke but I've seen it in clear Carnival as well as green.

#9

This little Imperial cutie is very nice, especially when found on a rich smoky color with golden highlights. Of course, it is also known on marigold, and I suspect green is a possibility. While the pattern is relatively simple - a series of arches filled with small hexogonal buttons - it is quite effective. Sometimes called Tulip and Cane, #9 is also found in wine, claret, and goblet shapes.

#270

Made by the Westmoreland Company, this cute little open-stemmed bowl is found in peach opalescent milk glass as well as the aqua color shown. It is a simple but effective pattern well worth collecting.

Nu-Art Chrysanthemum

Nu-Art (Homestead)

#5

#4

#9

#270

OCTAGON

Next to the Fashion pattern, this is probably Imperial's most common near-cut design, especially when found in marigold. But dark colors show up now and then, and the shape shown is rare in marigold. In the beautiful purple, the toothpick is extremely rare. Octagon is found in table sets, water sets, wine sets, footed vases, milk pitchers, goblets and rare toothpicks. It is a pleasing all-over pattern.

OCTET

Even if this pattern were not marked, we would attribute it to the Northwood Company because the exterior pattern is the Northwood vintage found on the Star of David and Bows bowl. Octet is also a dome-footed bowl, usually about 8½″ in diameter. It is a simple, but effective pattern - one that wouldn't be easily confused with others. The colors are marigold, purple, green, white and ice green. The purple is the most common.

OHIO STAR

This beautiful near-cut vase is almost 10″ tall and certainly is a stand out in the carnival vase field. While the majority of vases are of simple design, this one flaunts its multi-cut pattern even to the star in the high domed base. The coloring is excellent and not only is Ohio Star found in the usual marigold, green, purple but is reported in a beautiful blue! Certainly Millersburg blues are not easily found and one of these would enhance any collection. A rare compote is known.

OLYMPIC COMPOTE

The Millersburg Olympic miniature compote is **extremely** rare. Its measurements are the same as the Leaf and Little Flowers compote made by the same company, and the exterior and base are identical also. If ever the old adage "Great things come in small packages" could apply, certainly it would be to the Olympic Compote.

OMNIBUS

This interesting tumbler has been credited to the U.S. Glass company and is rather rare (six known) and little recognized. The primary design is a sunburst teamed with two diamonds of file and a pulled diamond of bubble-like filler, along with fanning. The sunburst moves from top to bottom in a series around the tumbler. The design is quite good, the color super. A rare find.

OPEN EDGE BASKET

This rather common Fenton pattern is found quite frequently in several sizes and colors, especially blue, marigold, green and amethyst. But pink, ice blue, ice green, white and red examples do exist in variously shaped items including hat shapes, vase whimseys, banana boat whimseys and bowl shapes. The interior may be plain or carry the Blackberry pattern and sometimes advertising is present.

Omnibus

Octagon

Octet

Ohio Star

Olympic Compote

Open Edge Basket

OPEN ROSE

This pattern is very similar to the Lustre Rose pattern but is not found on the wide range of shapes as the latter. The plate shown is the most sought shape but there are also footed and flat bowls of many sizes available. Colors of marigold, smoke, green, purple, clambroth and amber are known and each is usually outstanding. The amber plate shown typifies the Imperial quality.

OPTIC (IMPERIAL)

Each panel in this pattern is curved, thus the name and an interesting design above the ordinary. Besides bowls and small compotes, a creamer and sugar are known in marigold and smoke.

OPTIC AND BUTTONS

In crystal, this pattern is found in many shapes, including table sets, plates, oil bottles, decanters, shakers and sherbets, but in Carnival glass, Optic and Buttons is limited to berry sets, a goblet, a large handled bowl, a small pitcher, tumblers in two shapes and a rare cup and saucer. Many of the items in Carnival are marked with the Imperial "iron cross" mark, including the milk pitcher and the cup. All shapes I've seen are in marigold only.

OPTIC FLUTE

This Imperial pattern is seldom mentioned but can be found on berry sets as well as compotes. Colors I've seen are marigold and smoke but others may have been made.

ORANGE PEEL

This is a sister design to the Fruit Salad pattern and both are made by Westmoreland. Orangle Peel, while not as rare, is made in a punch set, custard set and a stemmed dessert in marigold, amethyst and teal, all Westmoreland prime colors.

ORANGE TREE

No other Fenton pattern had more popularity or was made in more shapes than the Orange Tree and all its variants. Known in berry sets, table sets, water sets, ice cream sets, breakfast sets, compotes, mugs, plates, powder jars, hat-pin holders, rose bowls, a loving cup, wines, punch sets and goblets. Orange Tree is found in marigold, blue, green, amethyst, peach opalescent, milk glass lustered, aqua opalescent, white, amber, vaseline, aqua, red and amberina.

ORANGE TREE AND SCROLL

What a beauty this hard to find tankard set is. The Orange Trees are like those on the regular pieces and the Orange Tree Orchard set, but below the trees are panels of scroll work much like the design on the Milady pattern. Colors are marigold, blue and green but I wouldn't rule out amethyst or white on this Fenton product.

Optic (Imperial)

Open Rose

Optic and Buttons

Optic Flute

Orange Peel

Orange Tree

Orange Tree and Scroll

ORANGE TREE ORCHARD

Obviously a spin-off pattern of the Orange Tree, this rather scarce Fenton water set has a nicely shaped bulbous pitcher. The design is a series of Orange Trees separated by fancy scroll work and has been reported in marigold, blue, green, amethyst and white.

ORIENTAL POPPY

Here is a very impressive, realistic pattern, especially effective on the chosen shape - a tankard water set. The mold work on this Northwood product is clear and clean and the glass is quality all the way. Colors are marigold, green, purple, white, ice green, ice blue and blue.

OSTRICH CAKE PLATE

This Australian pattern is actually the Emu on a footed cake stand, but has been misnamed. The exterior is a beautiful Rib and Cane pattern. Colors are marigold and purple but these are rare.

OVAL AND ROUND

While Imperial's Oval and Round may certainly be thought of as a very ordinary pattern, it does have its own charm on a bowl as nicely ruffled as the one shown. Simple in execution, the pattern is found on plates of large size and bowls of various sizes only. The colors are marigold, green or purple and are usually very richly lustered.

PALM BEACH

Apparently this U.S. Glass pattern was carried over from the pressed glass days. It is scarce in all shapes but can be found in a variety of useful pieces, including berry sets, table sets, a cider set, rosebowls, vase whimseys, a plate and a miniature banana bowl whimsey. The color is often rather weak and marigold, purple and white are known. The example shown is a bowl whimsey with an iridized "goofus" finish.

PANELLED DANDELION

Fenton's Panelled Dandelion is another of those spectacular tankard water sets that are so eye-catching. The panels of serrated leaves and cottony blossoms are very realistic and fill the space allowed nicely. Colors are marigold, blue, green and amethyst.

Orange Tree Orchard

Oriental Poppy

Ostrich Cake Plate

Oval and Round

Palm Beach

Panelled Dandelion

PANELLED HOLLY

This Northwood pattern is found in crystal, gilt glass and Carnival glass. However, the range of shapes is much less in the latter, limited to the exteriors of bowls, footed bon-bons, a rare breakfast set, and an extremely rare water pitcher. While fairly attractive, Panelled Holly is really not a great pattern. It appears a trifle busy, a bit confused. The most often seen color is green but purple and marigold do exist, and I've seen a combination of green glass with marigold iridescence.

PANELLED SMOCKING

I've always felt this pattern was from either England or Australia, but I may be wrong on both counts. Marigold is the only color I've seen, and there are no other shapes reported.

PANELLED TREETRUNK

While similar to the Northwood Treetrunk vase, this scarce and interesting vase has an appeal all its own. The example shown is 7½″ tall and has a base diameter of 4⅞″. It has eight panels, and the coloring is a fine amethyst. I suspect it was made by Dugan but can't be positive.

PANSY

The Pansy bowl shown typifies the Imperial quality so often found in iridized glass. The lustre is outstanding with a gleaming finish equal to the best Millersburg we all treasure so much. The mold work is super, enhanced by the very rich gold finish. While the Pansy pattern doesn't bring top dollar, it is a pleasure to own such a beautiful item.

PANTHER

One of Fenton's favorite animal patterns, Panther is realistic and found in footed berry sets. The small bowls in marigold are available, but the Master bowls, especially in darker colors are scarce. The example shown is a rare green, but Panther is known in marigold, blue, green, amethyst, red and a very rare white.

PARLOR PANELS

If you haven't had a chance to see one of these beautiful 4″ vases, especially the Imperial purple shown, you've certainly missed a real experience, for these are a glass collector's dream. Parlor Panels was shown in old Imperial catalogs and has not be reproduced to date. I've heard of marigold ones and I'm sure smoke and green are possibilities. Some examples are swung to 12″ lengths.

PASTEL PANELS

Usually found in pitchers and tumblers, we show a handled mug in this nicely done pattern. As you can see, the coloring is a very strong ice green, but this pattern is available in other pastels as well. I suspect Imperial to be the maker but can't be sure.

PEACH

Once more we show a Northwood pattern that was also produced in other types of glass. This was more than likely one of the earlier Northwood Carnival glass patterns and is found in a very fine cobalt blue as well as white, the latter often with gilting. What a shame more shapes were not made in peach, for only berry sets, table sets and water sets are known. The pattern is scarce and always brings top dollar.

PEACH AND PEAR

While no shards of this pattern were catalogued from the Dugan digs, I'm convinced it was their product. It is available mostly in marigold with an occasional amethyst one turning up. The mold work is excellent and only the one shape and size are known.

Panelled Treetrunk

Pastel Panels

Panelled Holly

Pansy

Panther

Panelled Smocking

Parlor Panels

Peach

Peach and Pear

PEACOCK (MILLERSBURG)

While both Fenton and Northwood had similar patterns, the Millersburg Peacock is most noted and by far the best example of this design. The detailing is considerably greater, the bird more realistic and the quality of glass and finish superior. There are slight differences between the large bowl and the individual berry bowls in the Peacock pattern, but most of these are in the detail permitted on the allowed space and a complete berry set is worth searching for. The color most often seen is a fine fiery amethyst, but green, marigold and clambroth exist as well as blue.

PEACOCK AND DAHLIA

While this Fenton pattern is related in design to the Peacock and Grape, it is a better design and much scarcer. Known only in bowls and plates, Peacock and Dahlia carries the Berry and Leaf Circle pattern on the exterior. Colors known are marigold, blue, green, amethyst, vaseline, white and aqua.

PEACOCK AND GRAPES

Obviously, this Fenton design and Peacock Dahlia were from the same artist. This too, is found on bowls, flat or footed, and scarce plates. Colors are marigold, blue, green, amethyst, aqua, vaseline, white, red and peach opalescent.

PEACOCK AND URN (FENTON)

The Fenton version of this pattern (both Northwood and Millersburg had their own) is most often seen on stemmed compotes in marigold or aqua. Other shapes are bowls, plates and a scarce goblet from the compote mold. Colors known are marigold, blue, green, amethyst, white, aqua, lavender and red.

PEACOCK AND URN (MILLERSBURG)

Millersburg Peacock and Urn differs from the regular Peacock pattern in that it has a bee by the bird's beak. The shapes known are large bowls or small 6½″ bowl, a chop plate, and a giant compote in the usual colors of marigold, green and amethyst.

PEACOCK AND URN (NORTHWOOD)

This subject must have been very appealing to the mass market for not only did Northwood have a version of Peacock and Urn but so did Fenton and Millersburg. And while there is little chance to confuse the Fenton version with the others, the Millersburg and Northwood patterns are quite similar. The Northwood Peacock and Urn is most often found on ice cream sets, has three rows of beading on the urns, and has more open space between the design and the outer edges of the bowl. Colors include both vivids and pastels as well as aqua opalescent. Shown is the rare 6″ plate in marigold.

PEACOCK AND URN "MYSTERY" BOWL (MILLERSBURG)

There is little mysterious about this bowl any longer. It is indeed from Millersburg, has a bee, two rows of beading on the urn and is found in both the ruffled and ice cream shape in 8″ and 8½″ diameters. Colors are the usual marigold, amethyst and green and all are rare.

PEACOCK AND URN VARIANT (MILLERSBURG)

Over the years, so much controversy has arisen over all the Millersburg Peacock designs, I'm showing all of them including this 6⅛″ very shallow bowl. Note that there is a bee and the urn has three rows of beads! The only color reported on this piece is amethyst and so far, four are known so it is rather rare.

Peacock and Urn "Mystery Bowl"

Peacock and Urn Variant

Peacock

Peacock and Dahlia

Peacock and Grapes

**Peacock and Urn
(Fenton)**

Peacock and Urn (Millersburg)

**Peacock and Urn
(Northwood)**

151

PEACOCK AT THE FOUNTAIN

Peacock at the Fountain probably rates as Northwood's second most popular pattern, right on the heels of the famous Northwood Grape, and it's so easy to see why. It is an impressive, well done pattern with an intriguing design. Available in berry sets, table sets, punch sets, water sets, compotes and a large footed orange bowl, Peacock at the Fountain was made in a host of colors, including the much prized ice green and aqua opalescent. Shards of this pattern were found at Dugan, leading us to believe Harry Northwood "farmed out" work to the Dugan Glass Company to keep up with demand on his best selling patterns. Dugan made a copy cat water set to be sure.

PEACOCK GARDEN VASE

This beautiful, well iridized vase was an early product of Northwood Carnival Glass and when the Northwood factory closed, many of the molds were purchased by the Fenton Company - thus, the reason this vase was re-issued by the Fenton Company a few years back in the other types of glass. At any rate, the Northwood Peacock Garden vase is truly a rare and beautiful sight to behold and a real treasure for the owners. The coloring is exceptional.

PEACOCK LAMP

This beautiful lamp base is on a crystal base glass, but with an enameled interior and an iridized exterior. Colors are marigold, smoke, amethyst and red. Occasionally there is no hole in the bottom indicating it was intended as a vase. Its height is 10¼", and sometimes it is found with a wooden base.

PEACOCK TAIL

Very reminiscent of the Northwood Nippon pattern, Fenton's Peacock Tail is known on bowls of all sizes, bonbons, compotes, hat shapes (some with advertising) and vase interiors. Colors I've seen are marigold, blue, green, amethyst, amber and red.

PEACOCK TAIL AND DAISY

I am very thrilled to finally show this very rare Fenton bowl pattern. Besides the marigold, there is an amethyst and a blue opal milk glass that isn't iridized, but I've heard of no other shapes or colors. As you can see, the pattern is graceful as can be, and the design is very well balanced.

PEACOCK TAIL VARIANT

One look at the iridescence of this little compote, and it becomes quite obvious it is a Millersburg product, culled from three common motifs used by most glass companies of the day - the peacock tail rings, the stippled rays and the feather. At any rate, it is a nice little item and quite enjoyable to own. Amethyst seems to be the most often seen color but marigold and green are known.

PEACOCK VARIANT (MILLERSBURG)

This extremely rare 7½" (same size as the Courthouse bowls) variant is an outstanding example of Millersburg craftsmanship. The mold work is very sharp with great detail and there is a bee, but no beading. Also the urn is quite different than the other peacocks. Colors are marigold, green and amethyst, but blue may exist.

Peacock Tail and Daisy

Peacock at the Fountain

Peacock Garden Vase

Peacock Lamp

Peacock Tail

Peacock Tail Vt.

Peacock Vt. (Millersburg)

PEACOCKS

Often called "Peacocks on the Fence," this Northwood pattern typifies what Carnival glass is really all about. An interesting pattern, well molded, and turned out in a variety of appealing colors, Peacocks is a delight. Only average size bowls and plates are known, but the color range is wide, including vivid colors, pastels and a really beautiful aqua opalescent. The exterior usually carries a wide rib pattern.

PEBBLE AND FAN

This very attractive vase is 11½″ tall with a base diameter of 4½″ and is truly a triumph. The mold work as well as the basic design is quite good. Colors I've heard about are cobalt blue, marigold and a rather unusual amber with vaseline finish.

PEBBLES (DUGAN)

Here is the Dugan version of Coin Dot and as you can see, it has no stippling. Found on open bowls and plates, colors are amethyst, marigold and green.

PENNY MATCH HOLDER

Once again we picture a rare but useful novelty that is seldom found. The octagonal base is 3⅜″ across and the entire Match Holder is 3½″ tall. Purple is the only color I've heard of, and the iridescence is very rich and heavy, very much like the better Northwood products in this color, but the maker remains unknown.

PEOPLE'S VASE

We are told this masterwork of art glass was produced by the Millersburg Company to show appreciation for the help of the Amish people of the area in getting the factory started. The dancing figures represent Amish children, hands clutching, prancing happily in thanks for a successful harvest - the only time their religion permitted such merriment. In the background, Grandfather looks on with pleasure. But regardless of the circumstances surrounding the vase's conception, there is no doubt that this is at the very top of Millersburg's best and surely deserves a place in the history of American glass. The only pattern variation occurs in the lip which is usually straight but very occasionally appears in scallops. The vase is 11½″ high, 5½″ in diameter and weighs 5 lbs. The colors are marigold, amethyst, green and cobalt blue.

PERFECTION

This beautiful water set is a fitting companion to its sister design, the Gay 90's. Outstanding moldwork, color and iridescence are the hallmark of Millersburg and the Perfection pattern certainly fits this description. The pitcher is 9½″ tall and quite bulbous. It has four mold marks. The tumblers are 4″ tall and taper from 2⅞″ diameter at the top to 2⅛″ at the base which has a 24 point rayed star.

PERSIAN GARDEN

Found in berry sets, ice cream sets and two sizes of plates, this very well designed pattern came from the Dugan factory. It is available in marigold, amethyst, green, blue, white, ice blue and ice green.

Pebbles (Dugan)

Peacocks

Pebble and Fan

Penny Match Holder

People's Vase

Perfection

Persian Garden

PERSIAN MEDALLION

Very oriental in flavor, Persian Medallion is one of those well-known Fenton patterns that was extremely popular when it was made and is available on bowls of all shapes and sizes, plates both large and small, compotes, rose bowls and even a hair receiver (not to mention interiors on punch sets). Colors are marigold, blue, green, amethyst, white amber and red.

PETAL AND FAN

Found only in bowls of various sizes, this Dugan pattern also has the Jeweled Heart as an exterior design. The motif itself is simple but attractive: a series of alternating stippled and plain petals on a plain ribbed background with a fan-like design growing from each plain petal. The feeling is almost one of ancient Egypt where such fans were made of feathers. Petals and Fans is available in many colors including peach opalescent.

PETER RABBIT

Peter Rabbit is one of Fenton's rare treasures, much sought by collectors and always priced for top dollar when sold. The shapes are 9" bowls and 10" plates in marigold, honey amber, green, blue and amethyst. The design is closely related to both Little Fishes and Coral patterns.

PICKLE PAPERWEIGHT

Of all the oddities I've come across in Carnival glass, this is probably the oddball of all time. It measures 4½" in length and is hollow. As you can see, it has a super color and finish. I assume it to be a paperweight for I can think of little else it could be used for. The maker is unknown, and the only color reported is amethyst.

PILLAR AND FLUTE (IMPERIAL)

Like so many good basic patterns from the Imperial Company, this simple design of narrow flutes has great balance by echoing these same flutes on the base in a pretty mirror-image. The color is good strong marigold on the bowl only.

PILLOW AND SUNBURST

This pattern is credited to the Westmoreland Company and while it has been seen on several shapes in crystal, the only reported iridized shape is the bowl shape. The pattern is exterior and can be found in marigold or purple. The example shown is an 8½" bowl.

PIN-UPS

This scarce Australian pattern, simple but distinctive, is found mostly on 8½" bowls in a rich purple, but here we show a very scarce marigold. The exterior carries a slender thread border.

PINCHED SWIRL

We seldom hear much about this attractive design, but it is known in both rosebowls and a rare spittoon, both in peach opalescent. I don't believe the maker has been confirmed, but Dugan or Westmoreland seem likely candidates.

PINE CONE

What a little beauty this design is! Known only on small bowls and scarce plates, Fenton's Pine Cone is seen mostly on marigold, blue or green, but an occasional amber plate has been seen. The design is well molded, geometrically sound, and the iridescence is usually quite good.

Pillar and Flute (Imperial)

Pickle Paperweight

Persian Medallion

Petal and Fan

Peter Rabbit

Pinched Swirl

Pillow and Sunburst

Pin-Ups

Pine Cone

PINEAPPLE

Sometimes called Pineapple and Bows, this Sowerby pattern is available in 7½" dome-footed bowls, a compote and a creamer. The mold work is quite good with much attention paid to detail. The luster is very good on the items I've seen and colors of marigold, purple and blue are known.

PINWHEEL VASES

Now known to be of English origin, these pretty vases are found in three sizes in colors of marigold, blue and amethyst. The mold work and coloring are very good and so is the design. Originally this pattern was called Derby.

PIPE HUMIDOR

Here is a fantastic Millersburg pattern many collectors haven't even seen because it is just that rare. And what a pity so few of these are around since it is lovely enough to grace any collection. The coloring and iridescence are exceptional and the design flawless. Imagine how difficult to remove the lid from the mold without damage to the pipe and stem. The humidor is just over 8" tall and measures 5" across the lid. A three-pronged sponge holder is inside the lid, intended, of course, to keep the tobacco moist. Around the base is a wreath of acorns and leaves above another leaf like pattern that runs down the base.

PLAID

On the few occasions this Fenton pattern is found, the coloring is usually cobalt blue with heavy lustre. The example shown is a rare red. As you can see, the coloring is very bright with rich iridescence. Needless to say, these 8½" bowls are a collector's dream and certainly would compliment any collection of red Carnival glass.

PLAIN JANE (IMPERIAL)

About all this Imperial bowl has going for it is the beautiful smoke finish and the radium luster, for the interior has no pattern and the back has only a wide panel with a star base. Still it is somehow special.

PLAIN JANE BASKET

Long credited to the Imperial Company, this large basket, while rather plain, has great appeal. It has been seen in smoke as well as marigold and measures 9¼" to the top of the handle.

PLAIN PETALS

Here is a pattern seldom discussed, yet it is found as the interior design of some pieces of Leaf and Beads. It is my opinion the latter was made by both Northwood and Dugan, and these pieces with the Plain Petals interior as well as the famous rosebowl are Northwood. The example shown is on a very interesting leaf shaped nappy.

PLUME PANELS

For years I felt this rather stately vase was a Northwood product but as you can see, it has been found in a beautiful cherry red so I'm rather sure it came from the Fenton factory. Other colors known are marigold, blue, green, amethyst and white.

Plain Jane (Imperial)

Plain Petals

Pineapple

Pinwheel Vases

Pipe Humidor

Plaid Bowl

Plain Jane Basket

Plume Panels

POINSETTIA (IMPERIAL)

Found only on one shape (the beautiful milk pitcher shown), Poinsettia is an outstanding Imperial pattern. Standing 6½″ tall, the Poinsettia is usually found in marigold or smoke color, but as you can see, a rare and beautiful purple does exist as does an equally rare green. What a shame more shapes do not exist in this beautiful design!

POINSETTIA (NORTHWOOD)

For some reason, in years past, someone attributed this very stylish pattern to the Fenton Glass Company. Just why, I can't guess, for Poinsettia was made by Northwood in custard glass and was illustrated in their advertising of the day. At any rate, this mistake has been corrected, and we now recognize this well done bowl as a Harry Northwood design. Poinsettia is found either as a flat based or footed bowl with the Fine Rib as an exterior pattern. The finish is nearly always superior. The colors are marigold, green, purple, fiery amethyst, white and ice green.

(INTERIOR) POINSETTIA

Here is something unusual - a tumbler with all the pattern on the inside. Of course, we've all seen the Northwood Swirl pattern which is also an interior one, but that was a simple geometrical design while the Interior Poinsettia is an offering of a large flower. Apparently these were never very popular for they are very scarce. Also, to the best of my knowledge, no pitcher has been found. The iridescence is on both the inside and outside and is a good rich marigold. Only some of these Northwood tumblers are marked.

POND LILY

Much like other Fenton patterns such as Two Flowers and Water Lily, Pond Lily has both scale filler and the Lotus-like flower. The only shape I've seen is the bon-bon, and colors reported are in marigold, blue, gree and white. Of course, other colors may exist and certainly red is a possibility.

PONY

For years the origin of this attractive bowl has been questioned and only recently has it been attributed to the Dugan Company. Colors seen are marigold, amethyst and ice green. The mold work is quite good.

POPPY (MILLERSBURG)

Large open compotes seem to have a fascination all their own, and this one from Millersburg is certainly no exception. It is quality all the way, whether found in green, purple or marigold. Standing 7″ tall and being 8″ across, Poppy has four mold marks. It often has the Potpourri as a secondary pattern. The poppy flowers and leaves are well done and are stippled.

**Poinsettia
(Imperial)**

**Poinsettia
(Northwood)**

Poinsettia Interior

Pond Lily

Pony

Poppy

POPPY (NORTHWOOD)

This Northwood pattern is most often found on small oval bowls, described as trays or, with the sides crimped, as pickle dishes. However, it is also found as an exterior pattern on larger bowls, some with plain interiors, others with a large Daisy in the center of the bowl. The colors are electric blue, marigold, peach, purple and white. Others may exist but these are the ones I've seen.

POPPY SHOW (NORTHWOOD)

Let me state from the beginning this is not the same pattern as the Poppy Show Vase. It is a beautiful well-made item, very much akin to the Rose Show pattern in concept and design. It is found only on large bowls and plates in a wide range of colors, including marigold, green, blue, purple, white, ice blue and ice green. This Northwood pattern brings top dollar whenever offered for sale.

POPPY SHOW VASE (IMPERIAL)

What a shame this beauty was chosen to be reproduced by Imperial in the 1960s! The old Poppy Show Vase is a real show stopper, standing about 12" tall, with a lip diameter of 6¾"! The mold work is very fine, with the graceful poppy in a series of four panels around the vase. I've seen this artistic gem in marigold, clambroth, pastel marigold, amber, green and purple. Naturally, the darker colors are quite scarce and are priced accordingly.

POTPOURRI (MILLERSBURG)

I certainly welcome the chance to show this very rare pitcher in the Potpourri pattern, a kissing cousin to Millersburg's Country Kitchen pattern. Only two of these pitchers have been reported and both are marigold, smaller than a water pitcher and were used for milk.

PRAYER RUG

Known only in the finish shown, beautiful custard glass with a marigold iridescence, Fenton's Prayer Rug is a seldom seen item. The only shape is a handled bon-bon, but I suspect time will bring to light additional ones since uniridized pieces are known in small bowls, vases and hat shapes.

PREMIUM

Not only found in the well-known candlesticks shown, but also in 8½" bowls, 12" bowls and 14" plates. Imperial's Premium pattern is shown in old catalogs in marigold, clambroth, purple, green and smoke. The candlesticks are 8½" tall, heavy and beautifully iridized! While not in the class with the Grape and Cable candlesticks, they are still quite nice. Used with the medium size bowl, they make a nice console set.

PRETTY PANELS

This is a marked Northwood tumbler and as such is quite a sight for tumbler collectors. The color is a very bold frosty green, and the enameled cherry design is above average. It is found in marigold also.

Potpourri (Millersburg)

Poppy

Poppy Show

Poppy Show Vase

Prayer Rug

Premium

Pretty Panels

PRIMROSE

For some reason, this Millersburg pattern hasn't received the "raves" it might, and I can't understand why. I have one and treasure it just as much as I do a Nesting Swan. The glass work is equally as good and the iridescence excellent. The reverse pattern is Fine Cut Hearts and the two blend beautifully. Primrose is found primarily on large bowls in the three main Millersburg colors, plus the spectacular blue shown.

PRIMROSE AND FISHNET (#2475)

This unusual Imperial pattern has two kissing cousins, also in red Carnival; one showing grapes, the other roses. The floral design is on one side only, and the fishnet covers the remainder of the glass. While red is the only reported color in iridized glass, all three patterns are known in crystal. The Primrose and Fishnet vase stands 6″ tall. Needless to say, they are quite scarce.

PRISM AND CANE

This very scarce product of Sowerby has an interior pattern of Embrossed Scroll variant and, as you can see, the base is ground. Apparently it is a sauce dish or jam dish as it measures 5″ across the rim and stands 2¼″ tall.

PRISM AND DAISY BAND

Apparently one of Imperial's late designs in Carnival glass and intended for a cheap mass sale, Prism and Daisy Band can be found only in marigold in berry sets, breakfast sets, a stemmed compote and a vase shape. The coloring is adequate but not superior.

PRISMS

We now have evidence to support a Westmoreland origin for this unusual little compote. For quite awhile, amethyst was the only color seen, but there is a marigold of which I've seen some four or five, and green also exists. Prisms measure 7¼″ across the handles and is 2½″ tall. The pattern is all exterior and is intaglio with an ornate star under the base like the one on the Cherry and Cable butter dish.

PROPELLER

Besides the usual small compote found in this Imperial pattern, I'm very happy to show the rare 7½″ stemmed vase in the Propeller pattern. The coloring is a good rich marigold, but others may exist since the compote is seen in marigold, green and amethyst.

Primrose

Primrose and Fishnet

Prism and Cane

Prism and Daisy Band

Prisms

Propeller

PULLED HUSK CORN VASE

Apparently Harry Northwood wasn't quite satisfied with this very rare example of a corn vase, for few of these are around in comparison with the regular corn vase. Known in two sizes, the Pulled Husk vase has been seen in green and purple and some are pulled more grotesquely than others.

PULLED LOOP

This rather simple Fenton vase design is found quite often, mostly in marigold, blue or amethyst, but it is known in a beautiful green, as well as an occasional peach opalescent finish. The size may vary from 8″ to 12″, but the finish is usually very heavily lustered.

PUZZLE

Found in stemmed bon-bons and compotes, Dugan's Puzzle is an appealing pattern. The all-over design is well balanced and the stippling adds interest. Colors known are marigold, purple, green, blue, white and peach opalescent.

QUEEN'S LAMP

I first showed this very rare lamp in my Millersburg book, and I still believe it came from that company. There are two green iridized ones known as well as a crystal example with a matching shade. The base of the lamp measures 7″ across and the lamp to the top of the font is 9½″ tall.

QUESTION MARKS

Here is a simple Dugan pattern found on the interiors of bon bons and occasionally compotes like the one shown. Again the exterior is usually plain, and the colors are peach opalescent, marigold, purple and white. Both the compote and the bon bon are footed; the compote is one of the small size, measuring 4½″ tall and 4″ across the highly ruffled edge. The exterior occasionally has a pattern called Georgia Belle.

QUILL

Once again we show a pattern of which shards were found in the Dugan diggings, and I truly believe Quill was indeed a Dugan Glass Company pattern. The pitcher is some 10″ tall and has a base diameter of 4½″. The colors are marigold and amethyst, and the iridescence is usually above average. Quill is a scarce pattern and apparently small quantities were made, again pointing toward the Dugan Company as the manufacturer. The water set is the only shape.

RAGGED ROBIN

Just why more of these Fenton bowls weren't produced is a mystery, but the fact remains these are quite hard to find today. Found only on average size bowls often with a ribbon candy edge. Colors reported are amethyst, marigold, blue, green and white with blue most available.

Queen's Lamp

Pulled Husk Corn Vase

Puzzle

Quill

Pulled Loop

Question Marks

Ragged Robin

RAINBOW (NORTHWOOD)

Just like the Northwood Raspberry compote or the one with only a Basketweave exterior, this one is completely plain with iridescence on the inside only. The luster swirls around the glass in layers, just like a rainbow, thus the name.

RAINDROPS

Here is another of the dome-footed bowls available in peach opalescent like so many offered by the Dugan Company. Remember, I said earlier that I felt Dugan was responsible for at least 90 percent of the peach Carnival, and a close study of these bowls will support this belief. Raindrops is found without stippling. It has the Keyhole pattern as an exterior companion and has four mold marks. All in all, it is a nice pattern to own, especially if you like the peach opalescent glass.

RAMBLER ROSE

Until quite recently, I'd always felt Rambler Rose was a Fenton product, but upon examining a large shard of this pattern from the Dugan dump site, I'm compelled to admit my mistake. This water set has a bulbous pitcher with a ruffled top. The flowers are well designed and clearly molded. The colors are marigold, purple, blue and green. Perhaps research in the years ahead will add more information about this pattern.

RANGER

Known in breakfast sets, water sets, a milk pitcher and table sets, this pattern, often confused with the Australian Blocks and Arches pattern, is found only in marigold. It is an Imperial product, but one version of the tumbler is known to have been produced by Christales de Mexico and is so marked.

RASPBERRY

Even without the famous trademark, this pattern would be recognized as a Northwood product, for it includes the basket-weave so often found on that company's designs. Available in water sets, table sets, berry sets and a milk pitcher. Raspberry has long been a favorite with collectors. The colors are marigold, green, purple, ice blue and ice green with the richly lustered purple most prevalent.

RAYS AND RIBBON

Each of the makers of Carnival glass seems to have had a try at a pattern using stippled rays. The Millersburg version is quite distinctive because of the bordering of ribbon-like design, resembling a fleur-de-lis design. Most of these bowls are not radium finish and usually carry the Cactus pattern on the exterior. Occasionally a plate is found in Rays and Ribbons, but one wonders if this were not produced as a shallow bowl. Amethyst is the usual color, followed by green, marigold, and vaseline in that order.

RIBBON TIE

Sometimes called Comet, this well-known Fenton pattern is found chiefly on all sorts of bowls as well as ruffled plates. The colors range from very good to poor in marigold, blue, amethyst, red and green, and often the luster is only so-so.

Rainbow (Northwood)

Raindrops

Rambler Rose

Ranger

Raspberry

Rays and Ribbons

Ribbon Tie

RIPPLE

This Imperial pattern is fairly common in marigold, clear or amethyst glass but the teal color shown is a real exception and quite a beauty. Ranging in height from 10″ to 16″, the Ripple vase depends on what design it has, in the "pulling" or "slinging" of the glass while hot and, naturally, the taller the vase, the less design exists.

RISING SUN

This very unusual pattern has been seen in both the marigold shown and cobalt blue. The pitcher is found in two variations, one with a pedestal base, the other flat base. A matching tray has been reported but I haven't seen it. The maker is U.S. Glass. A rare table set was made in marigold. Shown is the covered sugar.

ROBIN

Despite the reproductions of this fine old Imperial pattern, the prices have held up rather well on the old pieces. The water sets, found only in marigold, and the mug found in smoke are especially desirable. Apparently the appeal lies in the handsome presentation of the nicely done bird, the flower and branch dividers, and the flowering leaf pattern, so pleasing to the eye.

ROCOCO

This beautiful little Imperial vase was the first item in smoke I'd ever seen, and I must admit I loved it at first sight! While it may be found on a small bowl shape with a dome base and in marigold as well as smoke, it is the vase most of think of whenever Rococo is mentioned. The vase is 5½″ tall and shows four mold marks. I have had a green one reported but haven't seen it yet.

ROMAN ROSETTE GOBLET (UNLISTED)

While this pattern is not difficult to find in pressed glass, this is the only reported item in iridized glass to the best of my knowledge. As you can see, it is slightly crooked, but the iridization on the clear glass is unmistakable with beautiful blue and pink coloring. It measures 6″ tall and has a base diameter of 2¾″.

ROSALIND (MILLERSBURG)

Often called Drape and Tie, this classic Millersburg design is found as the interior pattern on Dolphin compotes, on rare 9″ compotes and large and small bowls. The colors are marigold, amethyst and green, but I've seen a 9″ bowl in a stunning aqua and a plate is known in green.

ROSALIND VARIANT (MILLERSBURG)

If you look closely at this design and the regular Rosalind shown elsewhere, you will see a good deal of difference, especially in concentric peacock tail sections. For this reason, I'm listing the compote shown as a variant (and expect letters about it). Colors reported in this compote are amethyst and green but marigold was probably made also.

Rosalind Variant (Millersburg)

Ripple

Rising Sun

Robin

Rococo

Roman Rosette Goblet

Rosalind

ROSE AND GREEK KEY PLATE

This very beautiful square plate is a sight to behold. Not only is it quite unique but so very well designed that I simply cannot understand why there aren't more of these. But alas, there's only the one known. The coloring is a smoky amber. The plate measures 8½" across, and the roses are deep and hollow on the underside, much like the well-known Rose Show bowls.

ROSE COLUMN

This stately Millersburg vase is a real beauty and like several Carnival patterns such as the Imperial Grape Carafe or the Grape arbor pitcher, the rows of roses are hollow. This require great skill by the worker when removing it from the mold, and many must have been broken in doing so. This lovely vase is 10" tall and 5" across the diameter. There are six columns of roses, each topped by a sprig of leaves. The iridescence is top-quality, and the colors are marigold, blue, green and amethyst. The Rose Column vase would make a lovely companion to the People's Vase.

ROSE GARDEN

Once again we finally have a true maker for a much disputed pattern, and Rose Garden is now in the list of glass from the Eda Glassworks of Sweden. It is found in many shapes including bowls, round and oblong vases, a pitcher that is rare, a beautiful rosebowl and a covered butterdish. Colors are marigold and blue only.

ROSE SHOW

What a handsome piece of glass this is! The design of this Northwood is flawless, heavy and covering every inch of available space. Yet it isn't in the least bit busy-looking. One has the distinct feeling he is looking into a reeded basket of fresh-cut roses and can almost smell the perfume. Found only on bowls and a plate variant, the beautiful pattern was produced in small amounts in marigold, purple, blue, green, white, ice blue, ice green, peach opalescent, amber, aqua opalescent and a rare ice green opalescent.

ROSE SHOW VARIANT

Over the years, very little has been learned about this plate variant of the Rose Show pattern, but as you can see, it is quite different in both flower and leaf arrangement and number. It is found in a host of colors including marigold, amethyst, green, blue, peach opalescent, aqua opalescent, ice blue and white.

ROSE SPRAY COMPOTE

Standing only 4½" at its tallest point, this beautiful compote is a real treasure. The only colors I've heard about are the beautiful ice blue and ice green. I suspect this is a Fenton product, but have no verification of this. The rose and leaf spray is on one side of the rim only and is rather faint, much like the Kittens bowls.

ROSE TREE

Make no mistake about it, this is a very scarce and desirable Fenton bowl pattern. I believe this was the Fenton answer to the Imperial Lustre Rose, but apparently it was made in small quantities. The colors known are marigold and cobalt blue, and the size is a generous 10" diameter.

Rose Show Variant

Rose and Greek Key Plate

Rose Column

Rose Garden

Rose Show

Rose Spray Compote

Rose Tree

ROSES AND FRUIT

This beautiful little compote is unique in several ways and is very hard to find Millersburg item. It measures 5¼″ from handle to handle and is nearly 4″ high. Notice the deep bowl effect (so often used by Millersburg on compote and bon bons) and the pedestal base. In addition, observe the unusual stippling around the edge of the interior, and, of course, the combination of roses, berries, and pears are quite distinctive. It is found in green and amethyst mostly, but was made in marigold and blue too.

ROSES AND RUFFLES LAMP (RED)

I'm frankly not too taken with Gone With the Wind Lamps, but the beautifully iridized ones are in a class by themselves, and the very few red ones known are simply beautiful. The Roses and Ruffles lamp is 22″ tall. It has excellent fittings of brass and is quality all the way. The mold work on the glass is quite beautiful and the lustre superior.

ROSETTE

Combining several well-known carnival glass patterns, including Stippled Rays, Beads and Prisms, this Northwood pattern isn't the easiest thing to find. In arrangement, it reminds one of the Greek Key pattern, but Rosette stands on its own. Found only on generous sized bowls, the colors are marigold and amethyst. Green may be possibility, but I haven't seen one.

ROUND-UP

As I stated earlier, Round-Up, Fanciful and Apple Blossom Twigs all have the same exterior pattern and shards of the latter two were found in the Dugan diggings. Found only on bowls, ruffled plates and true plates, Round-Up is available in marigold, purple, peach opalescent, blue, amber, white and a pale shade of lavender. The true plate is quite scarce and always brings top dollar.

ROYALTY

Perhaps one might mistake this for the Fashion pattern at first glance but with a little concentrated study, it becomes obvious they aren't the same. Royalty is a pattern formed from a series of hobstars above a series of diamond panels. Found on punch sets and two piece fruit bowls, this Imperial pattern is mostly found in marigold, but the fruit bowl set has been reported in smoke.

RUFFLED RIB SPITTOON

This little Northwood cutie could be called Fine Rib or Lustre and Clear I guess, but I feel the name given is more appropriate. At any rate, the coloring is a good rich marigold and the ribbing is on the interior. The spittoon stands 4″ tall and has a rim diameter of 4½″ with a collar base diameter of nearly 2″.

Roses and Fruit

Roses and Ruffles Lamp

Rosette

Round-Up

Royalty

Ruffled Rib Spittoon

RUSTIC

I would venture to say Rustic is one of the best known and most common of vase shapes for it is plentiful, found in many sizes and colors including marigold, blue, green, amethyst, aqua, vaseline, amber, white, peach opalescent and red. It was pulled from the Fenton Hobnail vase shapes and can be found in sizes from 6" to 20".

S-REPEAT

Made in crystal, decorated crystal, and gilt glass prior to being made in Carnival glass, S-Repeat is found in only a small range of shapes in iridized glass. Besides the punch set shown, there is a rare toothpick that has been widely reproduced and a handful of marigold tumblers that some believe are questionable. At any rate, in Carnival glass, Dugan's S-Repeat is a very scarce item.

SACIC ASHTRAY

This little ash tray is a real mystery in many ways. It reads: "NARAJA SACIC POMELO." Apparently it was meant to go to Brazil, but why an English glass maker would mold such an item escapes me. The color is quite good, with a touch of amber in marigold.

SAILBOATS

Found in small bowls, plates, compotes, goblets and wines. Sailboats is a well-known Fenton pattern that competes nicely with Imperial's Windmill pattern. Colors I've heard about are marigold, blue, green, vaseline, amber and red, but not all colors are found in all shapes.

SCALE BAND

While not too original, this Fenton pattern of smooth rays and bands of scale filler does quite nicely in the shapes chosen; bowls, plates, pitchers and tumblers. The color most seen is, of course, marigold; however, Scale Band can also be found in green, amethyst, peach opalescent, aqua opalescent (quite rare) and red.

FISH-SCALE AND BEADS

Most of these bowls I've seen are small - 6" to 7" in diameter. Nevertheless, they are well done, interesting items and add much to any collection. The Fishscale pattern is on the interior while the Beads design is on the exterior. When held to the light, one pattern fits happily into position to complement the whole, giving a pleasant experience.

SCARAB HATPIN

I have always avoided showing hatpins or buttons but the one here is so pretty, I couldn't resist. It is on a very deep amethyst base color and has super luster. It measures 1¾" x 1⅜".

Scarab Hatpin

Rustic

S-Repeat

Sacic Ashtray

Sailboats

Scale Band

Fish Scale and Beads

SCOTCH THISTLE

What a pretty pattern this is for the interior of a compote! As you can see, the exterior is plain like so many compotes but the edges have a very interesting ruffles effect. Colors I've seen are marigold, blue, green and amethyst but others may certainly exist. This pattern was manufactured by Fenton.

SCOTTIE

Surely there isn't a collector that hasn't seen these in the flea markets in scotties, poodles, bambis, duckies or rabbits. They are all covered powder jars, all marigold and made near the end of the Carnival glass heyday. Still the coloring is usually respectable, and they are cute little critters.

SCROLL AND FLOWER PANELS

I've always been intrigued by this stylish Imperial pattern even though it was reproduced in the 1960s with a flared top. As you can see, the mold work, while very busy, is quite satisfying and the coloring is super. I've seen this vase in marigold and purple, but green is a possibility. The vase stands 10″ tall on a collar base with a many-rayed star.

SCROLL AND GRAPE (MILLERSBURG)

Nothing pleases me more than showing an unlisted pattern, especially if it is Millersburg! The only example reported of this Multi-Fruits and Flowers punch bowl interior is such a find. From the center, four strings of acanthus leaves extend to four clusters of grapes, all topped by a rich scroll. What a shame this wasn't a standard pattern! It's as pretty as anything Millersburg ever made.

SCROLL EMBOSSED (IMPERIAL)

As I said earlier, while this pattern originated at the Imperial factory, it was later produced in England on Carnival glass, notably on the Diving Dolphins bowl and on a four-handled sauce dish. The Imperial Version is used with File pattern exterior on bowls, with Eastern Star as an exterior pattern on large compotes, as well as alone on bowls and smaller compotes. The usual colors are green, marigold or purple, but smoke does exist. A scarce plate shape is shown.

SCROLL EMBOSSED VT. (ENGLISH)

Much like its Imperial counterpart, this English version is found on small bowls, small handled ashtrays, compotes and the Diving Dolphins bowls. Without the exterior design, it would be impossible to say who made which. However, the English version is kown in marigold, blue, green and amethyst.

SEA GULLS VASE

This rare vase has been traced to the Eda Glassworks of Sweden, adding to their growing importance as a non-American maker of iridized glass. The only color reported is a rich marigold with a good deal of amber hue.

Scroll and Grape (Millersburg)

Interior of Scroll and Grape

Scotch Thistle

Scottie

Scroll and Flower Panels

Scroll Embossed

Scroll Embossed Vt.

Sea Gulls Bowl

Sea Gulls Vase

SEACOAST PINTRAY
Pintrays are not common in Carnival glass, and this one from Millersburg is one of the nicest ones. The irregular shaping, the beautiful coloring and fine detail make this an outstanding item. It measures 5½″ x 3¾″ and rests on an oval collar base. The colors are marigold, green, amethyst and a fine deep purple.

SEAWEED
Can you imagine a more graceful pattern than this one from Millersburg? The curving leaves and snail-like figures seem to be drifting back and forth in the watery depths and the bubbles of beading add just the right touch. Usually found on fairly large bowls, Seaweed has three mold marks. The colors are marigold, green and amethyst. Also a rare plate, and a rare small bowl have been found.

SEAWEED LAMP
I've heard of four of these lamps in two different base shapes, but all with the Seaweed design circling the body. All were in marigold ranging from quite good to poor. The example shown measures 12″ to the top of the font. The maker is unknown but the lamp is a rare one.

SHELL
I've always felt this was a superior Imperial pattern - simple yet effective. This is especially true on the few plates I've seen. The pattern is a well-balanced one of eight scalloped shells around a star-like pattern. The background may or may not be stippled - I've seen it both ways. The shapes are smallish bowls, plates and a reported compote I haven't seen. The colors are marigold, green, purple, smoke and amber.

SHELL AND JEWEL
Easily found, this Westmoreland pattern was made only in the shapes shown in colors of marigold, amethyst and green (white has been reported but not confirmed). The pattern is a copy of the Nugget Ware pattern of the Dominion Glass Company of Canada. Shell and Jewel has been reproduced, so buy with caution.

SHRINE CHAMPAGNE (ROCHESTER)
Shown is one of three known stemmed champagnes manufactured by the U.S. Glass Company, to be given away at Shrine Conventions (a rare toothpick is also known). The 1911 Rochester, New York Champagne has painted scenes of Rochester and Pittsburgh with gilt decoration. The other champagnes are the 1910 New Orleans and Tobacco Leaf (Louisville, Ky. - 1909). Each is a premium example of the glass maker's skill.

SHRINE NIAGARA FALLS
Every so often a little jewel comes to light, and I'm thrilled like a kid again. Such a find is this rare little toothpick holder. As you can see, it is a fine cobalt blue. One side has the Shrine emblem and the other says: "Brown, Nagle, Willock, McComb - Niagara Falls." The shape is that of a barrel giving added meaning and a touch of whimsey.

SILVER QUEEN
While this Fenton pattern has never been one of my favorite enameled water sets, it is certainly not all that easy to find and has good color and finish. It is found only in marigold with the wide silver band and white scroll and only in water sets.

Shrine Niagara Falls

Seacoast Pintray

Seaweed

Seaweed Lamp

Silver Queen

Shell

Shell and Jewel

Shrine Champagne (Rochester)

SINGING BIRDS

Found in custard glass, crystal and Carnival glass, Singing Birds is one of the better known Northwood patterns. The shapes are berry sets, table sets, water sets and mugs in vivid and pastel colors.

SIX PETALS

Nearly always seen in shallow bowls in peach opalescent, Six Petals is occasionally found in a rare plate. The other colors available are purple, green, blue and white. A Dugan product.

SIX-SIDED CANDLESTICKS

What a beauty this candlestick is! Not only is the near cut design quite imaginative, but the workmanship is just super. The Six-Sided Candlestick is 7½″ tall and has a base diameter of 3¾″. It has been seen in a rich marigold, an outstanding purple, smoke and green. It has been reproduced by Imperial in crystal, so be cautious in your selection!

SKI STAR

While this Dugan pattern is found occasionally on small bowls in purple, blue and green, it is on the larger dome-footed bowls in peach opalescent where the pattern has its "day in the sun." These are found in many variations, some crimpled with one side turned down, others with both sides pulled up to resemble a banana bowl. The exterior usually carries the Compass pattern, an interesting geometric design, or is plain.

LADY'S SLIPPER

Here's another novel miniature, so ornamental yet appealing. Needless to say, very few of these little cuties were ever iridized so all are rare. The Lady's Slipper is 4½″ long, 2¾″ high, and is a good marigold. The entire piece is covered with stippling. From U.S. Glass.

SMALL RIB

The compote shown has been pulled into the rosebowl shape but versions of the lip opened out are also known. Coloring is much like the Daisy Squares pieces and may have the same common maker.

Singing Birds

Six Petals

Six Petals

Ski Star

Six-Sided Candlesticks

Lady Slipper

Small Rib Compote

SMOOTH PANELS

While this Imperial design is very much like the Flute #3 pattern, there are small differences. The most obvious one is that the Flute panels are concave while the Smooth Panel ones are convex. Found in water sets in marigold, green and smoke, or an 11″ vase of pearl opalescent. This same vase has been seen in marigold, amber, smoke, green and purple. The example shown has the Imperial "iron cross" mark.

SMOOTH RAYS (WESTMORELAND)

Like most of the other major manufacturers, Westmoreland had a try at a Smooth Rays pattern in compotes and various size bowls with both flat and dome bases. Here is one of theirs in a beautiful blue milk glass iridized, but these were made in marigold, amethyst, green, marigold milk glass, amber and teal as well.

SNOW FANCY

Known in small bowls as well as a creamer and sugar breakfast set, this scarce near cut pattern is one not many collectors are familiar with. The bowl has been seen in green as well as a frosty white, and the breakfast set is shown in marigold; other colors may exist but I haven't seen them. It is a McKee product.

SODA GOLD

Much confused with Tree of Life and Crackle shown elsewhere in this book, Imperial's Soda Gold differs from either in that the veins are much more pronounced and are highly raised from the stippled surface. It is found only on short candlesticks, a rare 9″ bowl, and beautiful water sets in marigold or smoke.

SOLDIERS AND SAILORS (ILL.)

One of two known such commemorative plates, this is the Illinois version. It features the Soldiers and Sailors Home in Quincy, Ill. and measures 7½″. On the exterior is found Fenton's Berry and Leaf Circle design. The colors known are marigold, amethyst and blue.

SOUTACHE PLATE

I've long believed this to be a Northwood pattern, and while I've seen it on both bowls and lamp shades, this is the first footed plate I've run across. It measures 8¾″ in diameter and has peach opalescent edging. The foot is a dome base and is of clear glass.

SPIRAL CANDLE

Like the Premium Candlesticks also made by Imperial, these heavy, practical candlesticks were sold in pairs and were made in green, smoke and marigold. They measure 8¼″ from the base to the top, and as far as I know, did not have a console bowl to match. The smoke coloring is particularly beautiful with many fiery highlights.

Smooth Rays (Westmoreland)

Smooth Panels

Snow Fancy

Soldiers and Sailors (Ill.)

Soda Gold

Soutache Plate

Spiral Candle

SPIRALEX

This is the name used in England to describe these lovely vases so I've continued using it. The colors are marigold, amethyst, green and blue, and all I've seen are outstanding with very rich iridescence. Sizes range from 8" to 14".

SPLIT DIAMOND

I'm very happy to show the complete table set in this Davison pattern, for while the creamer is easily found, the covered butter and sugar is quite scarce in this country. The only color is a good strong marigold with fine luster and superior mold.

SPRING OPENING

Made from the standard Millersburg small berry bowl mold, this interesting hand-grip advertising plate is a seldom seen, always attractive item from the Ohio company. It measures 6½" in diameter, has the typical many rayed base and is known only in amethyst. The lettering says: "Campbell & Beesley Co. Spring Opening 1911."

SPRINGTIME

In many ways, this pattern is similar to Northwood's Raspberry pattern, especially since both are bordered at the bottom with versions of a basketweave. Springtime, however, is really its own master and bears panels of wheat, flowers and butterflies above and throughout the basketweave. Found in berry sets, table sets and very scarce water sets in marigold, green, amethyst and also in pastels, Springtime is a very desirable pattern.

SQUARE DIAMOND (COLUMN FLOWER)

Sometime after I gave this vase the above name, another author called it Column Flower so you have a choice. It was made at the Riihimaki Glassworks in Finland and has been seen only in blue.

STAG AND HOLLY

This is probably the best known animal pattern in all of Carnival glass other than the Peacock, and certainly it remains one of Fenton's best efforts. Often brought out at Christmas time, the Stag and Holly is found mainly on footed bowls, rare footed plates and rare rose bowls. Colors are marigold, blue, green, amethyst, aqua, peach opalescent and red.

STAR

While there may not be a great deal of inventiveness to this English pattern, it certainly serves a useful purpose and does it with a good deal of attractiveness. The clear center shows off the star on the base quite well, and the two tiny rows of rope edging add a bit of interest. Marigold is the only color I've heard about.

STAR AND FAN CORDIAL SET

This pattern is not the same as the vase with the same name, but has a close tie with the other cordial sets like Zipper Stitch which were made in Czechoslovakia. It is a rare grouping, the only complete set known.

STAR AND FAN VASE

I've been privileged to see the two Imperial marigold vases shown, but a beautiful cobalt blue example also exists, and it must be something, for the marigold ones are very beautiful examples of the glassmaker's art. The glass itself is thick and very clear. The lustre is rich and even, and the design is flawless. Star and Fan is 9½" tall.

Spring Opening

Square Diamond (Column Flower)

Star and Fan Cordial Set

186

Spiralex

Split Diamond

Springtime

Stag and Holly

Star and Fan Vase

Star

STAR AND FILE

Very much like Star Medallion in concept, Imperial's Star and File doesn't have the cane effect, but uses panels of file, hobstars and sunbursts in a well balanced design. Found in bowls, breakfast sets, a water set, a wine decanter set, handled vases, a rare rosebowl and a large compote, Star and File is known in marigold, smoke, purple and green.

STAR AND HOBS

This very attractive 9″ rosebowl has much to offer in both quality and looks. The color is a deep purple glass with beautiful gold luster and while the base pattern resembles Ohio Star, I believe this to be a European product.

STAR FISH

As you can see, this little compote is a real cutie. The design is strong and interesting, and the quality is top notch. Star Fish is from the Dugan Company and is seen in marigold, green, purple and the beautiful peach opalescent.

STAR MEDALLION

Star Medallion is a much overlooked, but well designed near cut Imperial pattern. Apparently, it was a very popular pattern in its day for it is found in many shapes, including bowls of all shapes, a table set, a handled celery, a 9″ plate, milk pitcher, punch cup, tumbler, goblet and a very beautiful compote. Colors are a rich marigold, smoke and occasionally a beautiful helios green.

STAR OF DAVID

For some unknown reason, only small amounts of this beautiful Imperial pattern must have been produced, for it is seldom seen today. As you can see, it is simply a Star of David half-stippled on a plain background with smooth ribbing to the edge of the bowl. The example shown measures 8¾″ in diameter and is the famous helios green of Imperial with a silver finish, but the pattern is also known in marigold, smoke and purple. The exterior carries the Arcs pattern.

STAR OF DAVID AND BOWS

The Northwood version of this figure (Imperial also produced a Star of David bowl) is a very attractive dome footed bowl and is a tribute to the Jewish religion. The Star is interlaced and is beaded while a graceful border of flowers, tendrils and bows edge the stippled center. The exterior is the Vintage pattern, and the colors are marigold, green and amethyst.

STAR SPRAY

Now and then this Imperial pattern is found in crystal or marigold Carnival glass; however, the smoke color is quite scarce, especially on the complete bride's basket. The bowl measures 7½″ in diameter and has a beautiful finish. The metal holder is nicely done, having a fine gold overspray and tiny rosettes with leaves on the handles.

Star and Hobs

Star and File

Star Fish

Star Medallion

Star of David

Star of David and Bows

Star Spray

STARFLOWER

I certainly wish I could provide a manufacturer of this rare and beautiful pitcher (no tumblers known) but I can't. Known in both blue and marigold, the pitcher has turned up in two heights. The mold work is outstanding and the design flawless. Please notice how much the design resembles that of Millersburg's Little Star pattern.

STIPPLED ACORNS

The covered candy dish shown comes rather late in Carnival glass production but is still attractive enough to be of interest. It stands 6½″ tall on a 3½″ footing. I've seen these in marigold, blue and amethyst, but don't know who made them.

STIPPLED DIAMOND SWAG

This beautifully designed English compote seems to be the only shape known in this pattern, and while Mrs. Presznick reports green and blue ones, I've seen only the rich marigold shown. The compote is 5″ tall and measures 5¾″ across the top, with a 3½″ base.

STIPPLED RAMBLER ROSE

Most trails seem to lead to the Dugan Company with this seldom-discussed pattern, but I have no proof they made it. The shape shown is the only one I've seen, and the colors are marigold and blue only.

STIPPLED RAYS (FENTON)

While Stippled Rays was used by both Northwood and Millersburg too, the Fenton version is perhaps the most commonly known and is available in bowls, bon-bons, compotes, plates, creamers and sugars. The colors found are marigold, amethyst, green, blue and a rare red.

STIPPLED RAYS (IMPERIAL)

As you can readily see, the Imperial version of Stippled Rays is quite different than that of the Fenton Company in that the edges are evenly scalloped and the pieces are footed. Known only in a breakfast set to date, I suspect other unreported shapes exist. The colors are marigold, smoke and helios green.

STIPPLED RAYS (NORTHWOOD)

Every Carnival-producing glass company had a stippled rays pattern, and it is probably the most common motif in the entire field of iridized glass other than the grape. Northwood had several versions. The one shown is a variant. The most unusual aspects of the bowl are the reversed N and the exterior pattern which is a Greek Key and Scales. As you can see, it is a beautiful fiery amethyst and the bowl is dome footed. Stippled Rays was made in most colors and several shapes.

Stippled Acorns

Starflower

Stippled Diamond Swag

Stippled Rambler Rose

Stippled Rays (Fenton)

Stippled Rays (Imperial)

Stippled Rays (Northwood)

STIPPLED STRAWBERRY

While this pattern has been reported previously in a tumbler only, it obviously wasn't limited to that shape, and it is a real pleasure to show this rare spittoon shape. It stands 3½″ tall and measures 4½″ across its widest part. The coloring is nothing spectacular but adequate. Along the spittoon's lip is a checkerboard pattern. The manufacturer is the Jenkins Company.

STORK ABC PLATE

I'm certain many collectors will question my placing this pattern as an Imperial one. But on close examination, this pattern and that of the Bellaire Souvenir bowl are almost identical in makeup. It is my guess both patterns were turned out late in the Imperial line and each are rather scarce. The only color is marigold.

STORK AND RUSHES

Stork and Rushes is another pattern whose shards were found in the Dugan diggings and since it has features that are typical of Northwood, I'm afraid it's difficult to state whether Dugan or Northwood made this pattern. At any rate, it is available in berry sets, punch sets, water sets, hats and mugs. I've seen only marigold, purple and blue with purple which is probably the hardest color to find.

STORK VASE

Much like the Swirl vase in concept, the Stork Vase was made by Jenkins and is usually found in a pale marigold glass. The Stork is on one side only, with stippling covering the other side. The Stork Vase stands 7½″ tall.

STRAWBERRY (FENTON)

This cute little bon-bon shape has been seen in all sorts of glass including crystal, custard, milk glass and Carnival glass where the colors range from marigold, cobalt, amethyst and green to the rare red amberina shown and a good rich all red. The design qualities aren't all that good, but the iridescence is usually adequate and on the whole, the Fenton bon-bon comes off nicely.

STRAWBERRY (MILLERSBURG)

Like its close relatives, Grape and Blackberry Wreaths this beautiful pattern is the culmination of the design. Its detailing is much finer than either of the other patterns and the glass is exceptional. The coloring is a true grape purple, and the iridescence is a light even gold. Like other Millersburg patterns, the shapes vary, but the deep tri-cornered bowl with candy-ribbon edge is my favorite. A rare compote exists in the usual colors.

Stippled Strawberry

Stork ABC Plate

Stork and Rushes

Stork Vase

Strawberry (Fenton)

**Strawberry
(Millersburg)**

STRAWBERRY (NORTHWOOD)

Available in only bowls of various sizes and plates in either flat or hand grip styles, this well-known Northwood pattern comes either plain or stippled. On the stippled version, there are three narrow rings around the outer edge; these are absent on the plain pieces. Colors are both vivid and pastel with the purple showing off the pattern to its best.

STRAWBERRY EPERGNE

The Strawberry Epergne is very much like the Fish Net one also made by Dugan; however the former is much rarer and has not been reported in peach opalescent yet. As you can see, the bowl exterior is plain and the base is domed.

STRAWBERRY SCROLL

Much like the rare Lily of the Valley in design, this rare Fenton water set is a real beauty that can stand along side of the best designs in Carnival glass. The shape, like that of the Blueberry set, is very artistic also. Colors reported are marigold and blue, but I suspect amethyst and green are possibilities.

STRAWBERRY INTAGLIO

I showed this pattern in my first glass book as a questionable Millersburg pattern. Since then we've been able to trace it to the Northwood Company through both a "goofus" bowl and a gilt decorated one, both bearing the famous trade-mark. The glass is thick, the design deeply impressed and the iridescence only so-so. I've seen large and small bowls only.

STREAM OF HEARTS

The same heart shape employed by Fenton on the Heart and Vine, and Heart and Trees designs is found here on the scale filler swirls that form a peacock's tail. Usually found on the compote shape, often with Persian medallion as an exterior companion, Stream of Hearts is available on a 10″ footed bowl also. Colors are marigold, blue and white.

STRETCH

While we couldn't take the time to show all the shapes made in Fenton's vase stretch line, I wanted to show these matching pieces because they so typify the Fenton style and because they are so scarce. Please note the contrasting colored handles are not iridized.

Strawberry

Strawberry Epergne

Strawberry Scroll

Strawberry Intaglio

Stream of Hearts

Stretch

STRUTTING PEACOCK

The only shapes in this Westmoreland pattern are the creamer and sugar and the only colors I've heard about are green or amethyst. The design is much like Shell and Jewel, also a Westmoreland product, but beware; these have been reproduced.

STUDS

Studs is found in a large tray, milk pitcher and footed juice tumbler. It is reported to be from Imperial, but I've always had a doubt about this. Marigold is the only color.

SUN-GOLD EPERGNE

Although I question the origin of this beautiful epergne, I don't for one minute doubt its desirability. The base is of highly polished pierced brass while the bowl and lily are of an unusual pinkish-marigold Carnival glass. The epergne is 12″ tall and the bowl has a 9¼″ diameter. The glass is clear and mirror-like and has good even iridescence.

SUNFLOWER

Sunflower must have been a very popular pattern in its day, for numerous examples have survived to the present time. It's quite easy to see why it was in demand. It's a pretty, well-designed Northwood pattern that holds iridescence beautifully. The bowl is footed and carries the very pleasing Meander pattern on the exterior. It is also found, rarely on a plate. The colors are marigold, green, amethyst and a rare teal blue.

SUNFLOWER AND DIAMOND

Long felt to be a Jenkins pattern, this well done vase is now known to be of Swedish origin and an example in blue has been reported. The usual color is a good marigold. The pattern is all intaglio and very deep.

SUNFLOWER PINTRAY

Like its companion piece the Seacoast Pintray, this Millersburg item joins the list of a select few. It is 5¼″ long and 4½″ wide and also rests on a collar base. The most unique feature is, of course, the open handle and the colors are marigold, purple, amethyst and a rich green.

SUNKEN HOLLYHOCK

Probably found more readily than the other "Gone With the Wind" lamps, Sunken Hollyhock can be found in marigold (often with a caramel coloring) and a very rare red. The lamp stands an impressive 25″ tall and certainly is a show stopper.

Studs

Strutting Peacock

Sun-Gold Epergne

Sunflower

Sunflower and Diamond

Sunken Hollyhock

Sunflower Pintray

SUNRAY COMPOTE

These small compotes, found on marigold over milk glass, are very pretty in their own plain way. Fenton made many such items, and I strongly feel this compote came from that company also.

SUPERB DRAPE

The title of this beautiful piece of glass is certainly appropriate - it is superb! About 6½" tall and 7" in diameter, this very rare vase is a true aqua with a rich even butterscotch iridization. The gently rolling top shows a mellow opalescence as does the base. All in all, this Northwood creation is a rare beauty that would grace any collection superbly!

SWAN, PASTEL

Of all the shards of patterns I catalogued from the Dugan dump site, I'm sure this pattern surprised me more than any bother. For years I considered these small novelties either Fenton or Westmoreland products with my vote leaning toward the latter. However, we now can say with some positiveness that they are Dugan. Found in pink, ice blue, ice green, marigold, peach and purple. The darker colors and peach are the scarcest and demand greater prices. A variant by Fenton is known.

SWEETHEART

Besides the rare and beautiful covered cookie jar shown, this Cambridge pattern is known in a very rare tumbler shape in marigold. The cookie jar has been seen in marigold, green and amethyst and as you can see, the mold work and finish are superior.

SWIRL (IMPERIAL)

This 7" vase is shown in old Imperial catalogs, and I've heard of it in marigold, smoke, green and white. The design is nothing outstanding, but the useful shape and the iridescence are adequate.

SWIRL (NORTHWOOD)

I've seen this pattern on a beautiful tankard water set and the mug shape in marigold. The tumbler is shown in the Owens book in green and is known in amethyst. While the tumblers are often marked, the mug isn't. Now and then, the tankard pitcher is found with enameled flowers added. Naturally the pitcher is scarce and the mug is considered rare.

Sunray Compote

Superb Drape

Swan Pastel

Sweetheart

Swirl (Imperial)

Swirl (Northwood)

SWIRLED FLUTE VASE

This cute little Fenton vase is a real charmer for such simplistic design. The wide panel is quite pronounced at the base and the color and iridescence are quite good. These little vases average about 9″ in height and are found in red, marigold, green, amethyst, blue and white.

SWIRL CANDLESTICK

This very attractive candlestick is the same pattern as the rare mug I showed in previous books and was apparently a product of either Northwood or Dugan. While other colors may exist, I haven't heard of any. The luster is top notch and the glass, quality all the way.

SWIRL HOBNAIL

This is a little Millersburg jewel in either the rosebowl or the ladies spittoon, and once you own either piece, wild horses couldn't drag it away. The glass is simply sparkling and the iridescence outstanding. The spittoon has an irregular scalloped edge opening and both shapes have a many rayed base. The usualy colors prevail, but the green is extremely difficult to locate. Swirl Hobnail can also be found in a vase shape.

SYDNEY

The rare Sydney tumbler shown is one of a handful known and is from the Fostoria Glass Company. The only color reported is marigold that tends toward a honey-amber tone. The four large ellipsed crosses around the tumbler are the main motif and this design is repeated on the tumbler's base.

TAFFETA LUSTRE CANDLESTICKS

These very rare Fostoria candlesticks were manufactured in 1916 or 1917 (according to an old Fostoria catalog) in colors of amber, blue, green, crystal or orchid. They were part of a "flower set" which included a centerpiece bowl 11″ in diameter. The candlesticks themselves came in 2″, 4″, 6″, 9″, 12″ sizes and as you can see, these still have the original paper labels on the bottom. When held to the light, the ultra-violet color is fantastic and the iridescence is heavy and rich. Fostoria made very small amounts of iridized glass and certainly these example of their Taffeta Lustre line are quite rare.

TEN MUMS

Found on beautiful water sets, large impressive bowls, and rare plates, Fenton's Ten Mums is a very realistic pattern. The mold work is unusually fine, especially on the bowl shape. Colors are marigold, cobalt blue, green, peach opalescent and white but not all shapes are found in all colors.

THIN RIB (NORTHWOOD)

Here is an exterior pattern every one must know for besides the famous basketweave, it is found on some of Northwood's best known bowl patterns, including Good Luck and Strawberry. It is simple enough but held to the light, it adds greatly to the design.

THIN RIB AND DRAPE

Much like the other Thin Rib vases, this one has an interior drape pattern, adding to the interest. It can be found in several colors including marigold, green and amethyst. I suspect Fenton is the maker, but can't be sure.

Thin Rib (Northwood)

Sydney

Swirled Flute Vase

Swirl Candlestick

Swirl Hobnail

Taffeta Lustre Candlesticks

Ten Mums

Thin Rib and Drape

THISTLE

Fairly typical of many Fenton bowl patterns, Thistle is artistically true with the thistles and leaves realistic and graceful. Found on bowls, plates and a rare compote, the colors seen are marigold, green, blue and occasionally amethyst. Now and then a bowl appears with advertising on the base.

THISTLE AND THORN

British in origin, this nicely designed pattern is found on a variety of shapes, all footed, including bowls, sugars, creamers, plates and nut bowls. Colors are usually marigold but I've had blue reported.

THISTLE BANANA BOAT

This beautiful Fenton banana boat is another of the underrated patterns in Carnival glass. Massive in concept, bold in design with the thistle on the interior and cattail and waterlily outside, the four-footed Banana Boat is usually found on marigold, green or cobalt blue. The iridescence is quite heavy, usually with much gold.

THISTLE VASE

What a pretty little vase this is. Standing 6″ tall with a soft amber shading to the glass, the Thistle vase is a well-designed bit of color for vase lovers. The maker is unknown.

THREE FRUITS

So very close in design to the Northwood Fruits and Flowers pattern shown earlier in this book, the two substantial differences are the absence of the small flowers and the addition of an extra cluster of cherries to this pattern. Found in bowls of all sizes, including flat and footed ones, and average size plates. Northwood's Three Fruits is available in all vivid colors as well as pastels.

THREE FRUITS MEDALLION

If you will look closely you'll see the differences between this pattern and the regular Three Fruits design, including the addition of flowers and leaf tendrils. The large bowl is footed, has a reverse pattern of Meander, and the one show is on black amethyst glass and is a real show-stopper.

THREE FRUITS VARIANT

If you'll compare this beautiful 9″ plate with the Northwood version, you'll see a good deal of similarities and some obvious differences. While this version has been credited to Fenton, I strongly suspect it was a Dugan product.

THREE-IN-ONE

Originally called "Number One" in the crystal line, this well-known Imperial bowl pattern (plates also exist) is always easy to spot because of the two rows of near cut diamond designs, separated by a center area of flutes. I've seen bowls in 4½″, 7½″, 8¾″ sizes, in colors of deep marigold, green, purple and smoke. The iridescence is usually quite good and the glass heavy, clear and sparkling.

Three Fruits Medallion

Thistle

Thistle and Thorn

Thistle Banana Boat

Thistle Vase

Three Fruits

Three Fruits Vt.

Three-In-One

THREE MONKEYS BOTTLE

I'm not sure how many of these are around but not many I'd guess. The one shown is the reported example in all the previous pattern books, so it may have only few brothers. The Three Monkeys bottle is of clear glass with **good** iridescence, stands 8″ tall and bears the words, "Patent Pending - 8 oz." on the base. A rare find for bottle lovers.

THREE ROW VASE

I was very impressed when I saw this beautiful Imperial rarity. The color was truly fabulous and the iridescence fine enough to rival the Farmyard bowl. I have heard of only this one piece in beautiful purple, but others may exist. It is 8″ tall and 4½″ wide, and the mold work is quite deep and sharp. There is also a variant called Two Row vase which is quite similar.

THUMBPRINT AND OVAL

Standing only 5½″ tall, this well-molded Imperial pattern is known in marigold and purple. Either color is scarce and Thumbprint and Oval is much sought.

THUNDERBIRD (SHRIKE)

Called Thunderbird in America, the bird shown is actually a Shrike. The flora is of course, wattle. This Australian pattern can be found in both large and small bowls in marigold or purple.

TIGER LILY

It really is a shame this well-done Imperial pattern was used only on the water set. It would have been quite effective on any number of other shapes, including table sets and punch sets. The mold work is some of Imperial's best, all intaglio, and very sharp and precise. Tiger Lily is found in marigold, green and rarely purple. It has been reproduced in pastels, so beware!

TINY COVERED HEN (LITTLE)

The Imperial novelty item shown is a really well-conceived miniature that until recently had not been reproduced; however, I saw one of these in a gift shop in blue glass (not Carnival) not long ago. At any rate, the one shown is old and rare. The coloring is a very nice clambroth, richly iridized with a fiery finish. It measures 3½″ long and 3¼″ tall.

TINY HOBNAIL LAMP

In all my years in collecting, I've seen just two of these miniature oil lamps even though they do come late in Carnival glass history. The base is 3″ high and has a diameter of 2¼″. The shade, which matches, is clear. I haven't a notion as to the maker, but they are scarce and cute as can be.

TOBACCO LEAF (U.S. GLASS)

Here is another souvenir champagne, but the one shown is a real rarity. Please note that the finish is GOLD, not the usual clear iridized! As the owner says, this must have been for someone very special at the convention.

TOMAHAWK

This lovely miniature (7¼″ long and 2″ wide) is a real "show stopper." Now known to have been a product of the Cambridge Glass Company, the rare Tomahawk is a very deep cobalt blue with heavy iridescence. It has been seen in pieces other than carnival glass and has been reproduced in aqua and vaseline glass, but as far as I know, no iridized reproductions were made.

Tiny Hobnail Lamp

Tobacco Leaf (U.S. Glass)

Three Monkeys Bottle

Three Row Vase

Thumbprint and Oval

Thunderbird (Shrike)

Tiger Lily

Tiny Covered Hen

Tomahawk

TORNADO

Perhaps because it is one of the most unusual vases in all of Carnival glass, Northwood's Tornado is always a favorite with collectors. Available in both plain and ribbed, the size may vary considerably, and I've seen a mini-version in marigold. The colors are marigold, green, purple, white and ice blue. The Northwood trade mark is found on the inside of the vase.

TORNADO VARIANT

This extremely rare variant is one inch taller than the regular Tornado vase. The base closely resembles that of Northwood's Corn Vase and the top is tightly crimped. The only color reported is a deep rich marigold, iridized both inside and out.

TOWN PUMP

Certainly there isn't one collector of Carnival glass who isn't familiar with this very famous pattern. The Town Pump is almost 7″ tall and is mostly on purple, although marigold and green are found in limited quantities. The design is simple but very pleasing - ivy twining over a stippled background with a crude tree bark spout and handle. No Carnival glass collection would be complete without this pattern and certainly it deserves a prominent place in any Northwood collection.

TRACERY

This pattern comes as quite a surprise to many Millersburg fans because of its delicate patterning, but Millersburg it certainly is. It is found on bon-bons of rather deep, oval shape and is usually seen in green or amethyst. It measures 7½″ long and 5½″ wide. The base is 3″ in diameter and has a many rayed center. The exterior is plain and has two mold marks.

TREE BARK

As you can see, this is a simplistic pattern, turned out as a giveaway item or an inexpensive. The only shapes I've heard of are water sets with either open or lidded pitchers and the only color is marigold, usually of a deep, rich hue. While it certainly does not show the artistry the Imperial Company was known for, Tree Bark does fulfill its purpose of being an available bit of color for the average housewife's table.

TREEBARK VARIANT

If you look closely, you can see this design is slightly different than the regular Tree Bark pattern, having grooves that are straight rather than random spaced. I've seen this on this small tumbler as well as an ornate candle holder with a fancy brass cherub and a marble base.

TREE OF LIFE

There has always been a great deal of confusion surrounding this pattern and Crackle and Soda Gold patterns because they are so similar, but there is really no need for the confusion. As you can see, Tree of Life has no stippling whatsoever, thus the filler area is plain. The pitcher shown is a scarce shape in this pattern, and as you can see, the iridescence is thin and light. The shapes known are water sets, plates and perfume bottles.

TREE TRUNK

Simple but effective is the bark-like pattern for this popular Northwood vase. Apparently it was a well-liked pattern when it was being manufactured for many examples exist in sizes from 8″ to tall 20″ ones. The colors are marigold, blue, purple, green and white.

TRIADS (AND TOWERS VASE)

Triads is a product of Sowerby and is found in a covered butter dish, creamer, super, celery and spooner (both shown). The only color reported is a good rich marigold. The other small hat shape shown is called Towers and is a vase pattern also from Sowerby.

Triads (and Tower Vase)

Tornado

Tornado Variant

Town Pump

Tracery

Tree Bark

Tree of Life

Treebark Variant

Tree Trunk

TRIPLETS (DUGAN)

This common Dugan pattern is probably seen as much as any by the beginning collector and must have been produced by the carloads. Colors are marigold, amethyst, green, peach opalescent and white but not all are good and some of the peach is downright awful.

TROPICANA VASE

The maker of this intriguing vase is unknown, but I suspect it may be English. It stands 9″ tall and has a very rich marigold coloring.

TROUT AND FLY

Of course, this is a companion piece to the Big Fish pattern and except for the added fly and a few changes in the water lilies and blossoms, is much the same. The bowls usually measure about 9¼″ in diameter and have a wide panel exterior. The detail is good and the coloring excellent. The shape may vary and even square bowls and a rare plate shape have been found in this Millersburg pattern.

TULIP (MILLERSBURG)

This beautiful and rare compote is exactly like the Flowering Vine one shown elsewhere except it has no interior design. It stands about 9″ tall and the bowl measures roughly 6″ across. The only colors I've seen are marigold and amethyst but green was more than likely made. In addition to this size, a 7″ variant is known in amethyst.

TULIP AND CANE (IMPERIAL)

Seldom found, this old Imperial pattern is seen in iridized glass only on two sizes of wine goblets, a claret goblet and a rare 8 oz. goblet, in marigold and smoke.

TULIP SCROLL (MILLERSBURG)

Only a few of these attractive Millersburg vases seem to show up from time to time, mostly in amethyst, but once in a while in green or the quite rare marigold. I've seen them as tall as 11″ but most are about 7″ and less stretched out. They are always quickly snatched up and are a popular vase pattern.

TWINS

Like Imperial's Fashion pattern, Twins is another geometric design manufactured in large quantities in berry sets, a rare bride's basket, and the familiar fruit bowl and stand. Pieces have been found in a good rich marigold and a very beautiful smoke and the berry set has been found in green, as shown. Needless to say, a purple fruit bowl and stand would be a treasure!

TWO FLOWERS

Once again the scale filler, water lilies, and blossoms are used by Fenton to form an artistic presentation. Known in footed and flat bowls of various sizes and a scarce rose bowl shape, Two Flowers is seen in blue, marigold, amethyst, green and occasionally white.

TWO FRUITS

Once this Fenton pattern was felt to be an Imperial product but we know from old adveriesments that it came from Fenton. The background is Fenton's Stippled Rays and, as you can see, there are four sections to the divided bon-bon. Each section contains one fruit - either a pear or an apple. Colors I've heard about are marigold, blue and amethyst but certainly green may exist.

Triplets

Tulip and Cane

Tropicana Vase

Trout and Fly

Tulip Scroll

Tulip (Millersburg)

Twins

Two Flowers

Two Fruits

TWO FRUITS

Here is a Northwood pattern so unique and so very rare, it is not listed in the two major pattern guides. Shown is the spooner in a rich cobalt blue. It last sold in the 1977 Wishard auction. I know of one other piece in this pattern, a lidless sugar. Shown is the cherry side; the other pattern on the opposite side shows two peaches. The spooner measures 6¼" x 4½" and bears the Northwood trademark.

UNSHOD

The owner says this pitcher came with tumblers in the Unshod pattern so we've listed the pitcher as that pattern. If anyone knows differently, I'm sure I'll hear about it. The styling looks very much like the Millersburg Cherry, but that's only an observation.

URN VASE

This unusually shaped vase has been seen in white as well as marigold Carnival glass and is a product of the Imperial Company. It stands 9" tall and has a finely grained stippling over the surface.

VENETIAN

While credited to the Cambridge company, there is evidence that this pattern was iridized at the Millersburg factory. It is shown in old Cambridge ads, however, and the vase was used as a lamp base. Colors are green and a scarce marigold. The base design is quite similar to the Hobstar and Feather rosebowl. A rare butterdish is shown in marigold.

VICTORIAN

This impressively large bowl is another pattern from the Dugan factory in Indiana, Pennsylvania and is both rich and desirable. Mostly found in a rich purple, one example in a rare peach opalescent has turned up and rates with the best of bowls.

VINEYARD

Here is another pattern whose shards I catalogued from the Dugan diggings, but actually it didn't come as too much of a surprise. The same design was made in 1905 in crystal, opaque glass, and opalescent wear under the name, Grape and Leaf. Known in iridescent glass, in a water set only, the colors are marigold, purple and rarely peach opalescent. Often the tumblers are poorly formed and the glass tends toward being bubbled.

VINING LEAF

There are two variants of this English pattern - one with small berries along portions of the stylized leaves. The examples shown, a rather small bud vase and an ample lady's spittoon, give us the pattern nicely. Please note the frosted effect around the leaves.

VINTAGE (FENTON)

Vintage was the Fenton Company's primary grape pattern, and as such can be found in a wide range of shapes, including bowls, plates, rose bowls, compotes, punch sets, ferneries and a one-lily epergne. Shown is the Vintage fernery in a rare red. Other colors known are marigold, blue, green, amethyst, amber, pastel marigold and amberina.

VINTAGE (MILLERSBURG)

What makes Vintage unique is the hobnail exterior (the hobnail and the honeycomb seem to have been patterns used as standard fillers by Millersburg). It has a many-rayed star in the base and is usually seen on the medium size, shallow bowls. The Millersburg Vintage pattern is a scarce one and is certainly a credit to any collection. Colors are green, marigold, amethyst and blue. And both 9" and 5" bowls are known.

VINTAGE BANDED

Often seen in the mug shape, this Dugan pattern is rather scarce in the footed pitcher shape, and the tumbler is rare and much sought. Please note the grapes are almost identical to those found on the Golden Grape pattern, and the banding is quite similar to that found on the Dugan pattern called Apple Blossoms.

Vintage (Millersburg)

Vintage (Fenton)   210

Two Fruits

Urn Vase

Venetian

Victorian

Unshod

Vineyard

Vining Leaf

Vintage Banded

VINTAGE LEAF (FENTON)

Over the years, I've never been able to accept this design with the center leaf as the standard Fenton Vintage pattern so I've given in to my conscience and given it a name all its own. It is found in berry sets in marigold, green, blue and amethyst and is Fenton, not Millersburg, despite the Radium finish.

VIOLET BASKETS

Here are two of the dainty little baskets designed to hold small bouquets like violets. One has its own glass handle, while the other fits into a handled sleeve. The File pattern in the glass is much like that on some Stork and Rushes pieces, and I suspect both of these baskets come from the Dugan Company.

VIRGINIA BLACKBERRY

Known to be a variant of a U.S. Glass pattern called Virginia or Galloway, this small pitcher has turned up on a child's water set in crystal without the berries. The example shown in blue Carnival is the only reported on that is iridized, making it a very rare item indeed.

VOLTIVE LIGHT

Also bearing the strange M-inside-a-C mark like Oklahoma, this very hard to find novelty has a beautiful marigold finish. It stands 4¼" tall and is a candle vase. The side shown is the Bleeding Heart of Jesus. On the opposite side is a raised cross measuring nearly 2" tall.

WAFFLE BLOCK

This Imperial pattern was originally made in many shapes. The pitcher is hard to come by and, of course, the tumblers are rather rare, but other shapes, including a handled basket, rose bowl, punch set, vases, bowls, parfait glass and shakers are known. Colors are marigold, clambroth, aqua and amethyst.

WATER LILY

Found on bon-bons and flat and footed berry sets, Water Lily is similar to Lotus and Grape, Pond Lily and Thistle and Lotus. They each give a feeling of a small lily pond. The usual lotus-like flowers are present along with water-lily blossoms, leaves and small vine-like flora. Colors known are marigold, blue, green, amethyst, amber, white and red.

WATER LILY AND CATTAILS (FENTON)

While both Fenton and Northwood had versions of this pattern, the Fenton one is best known and is available in more shapes, including water sets, table sets, berry sets and a rare spittoon whimsey. Colors are marigold and amethyst, but certainly blue or green may exist but have not been reported.

Vintage Leaf

Virginia Blackberry

Violet Baskets

Voltive Light

Waffle Block

Water Lily

Water Lily and Cattails

WATER LILY AND CATTAILS (NORTHWOOD)
Here is a pattern used in different degrees by both the Northwood and Fenton companies, and at times it's rather hard to tell who made what. The obvious Fenton rendition is the exterior pattern used on the Thistle banana boat, but it is believed they made other shapes in Water Lily and Cattails, including a whimsey toothpick. This is the Northwood water set.

WATER LILY AND DRAGONFLY
This large (10½") shallow bowl and matching frog is called a flower set and was used much like an epergne. A large flannel flower is under the frog. In Australia these are also called "float bowls."

WHEAT
Make no mistake about it, this is a very rare Northwood pattern, known in only a covered sweetmeat (2 known) and a single covered bowl in colors of green and amethyst. Surfacing in Carnival glass circles only in the last 10 years, these rarities have caused much excitement and brought astonishing prices where they've been shown. The sweetmeat is the same shape as the Northwood Grape pattern. What a pity we don't have more of this truly important pattern.

WHIRLING LEAVES
What a simple but effective pattern for large bowls! Four flowing leaves and four star-like blossoms - what could be simpler. Please note that the flowers are very much like those found on the Little Stars bowls. This pleasing pattern is not especially difficult to find and does not sell for nearly as much as most Millersburg patterns but it is worth owning.

WHIRLING STAR
While this Imperial pattern had never brought many raves, it is a nice, well planned design found on punch sets, bowls and an attractive compote. Colors are mostly marigold, but an occasional piece in green is found.

WHITE OAK
After years of doubt about the maker of this rare tumbler (no pitcher known), I'm half convinced it was a Dugan product. The bark-like background and the general shape are much like the Vineyard tumbler. Of course, I could be wrong.

WICKERWORK (ENGLISH)
Sometimes only the bowl without the base of these is found, but here is the complete set. The bowl measures 8½" in diameter. The only color I've seen is the marigold. Apparently, this was a cookie or sandwich tray.

WIDE PANEL (IMPERIAL)
Like the other major Carnival glass companies, Imperial produced a Wide Panel pattern. These are found primarily in goblets of two sizes and a covered candy jar. Colors known are marigold, ice blue, ice green, vaseline white, pink and red. Most have a stretch effect around the edge.

Wickerwork (English)

Waterlily and Cattails

Water Lily and Dragonfly

Whirling Star

Whirling Leaves

Wheat

White Oak

Wide Panel

WIDE PANEL EPERGNE

This beauty is the most stately epergne in Carnival glass and is a product of the Northwood factory. Colors are white, marigold, green, amethyst and the ultra-rare aqua opalescent one shown.

WIDE PANEL VARIANT

Rather plain for a Northwood product, this water set relies on symetry and grace for its charm. It can be found in marigold and white as well as enameled in both colors and a beautiful persian blue.

WIDE PANELLED CHERRY

Unlisted until now, this very interesting pattern is similar to the Stippled Strawberry spittoon I showed in "Rarities In Carnival Glass" some years ago. The shape is a very small pitcher, possibly used for syrup or cream and to date I've heard of no matching pieces.

WIDE RIB VASE

While several glass companies produced these wide rib vases, the one shown came from the Dugan factory. Colors I've seen are marigold, green, blue, amethyst, smoke, white, amber, peach opalescent and aqua opalescent.

WILD BLACKBERRY

Very much in design like the other Fenton Blackberry patterns, this is strictly a bowl pattern easily identified by the four center leaves and the wheat-like fronts around the outer edges. Colors are marigold, blue, green and amethyst. The exterior has the wide panel pattern.

WILD FLOWER (MILLERSBURG)

This deeply cupped, clover-based compote is just over 6″ tall and is 4½″ wide. The very graceful pattern of four large leaves, four small leaves, and eight blossoms is quite effective. The iridescence is found only on the inside of the compote and has the usual radium finish. This is not an easy compote to find, and anyone having one should be proud. This Millersburg pattern is found in marigold, green, amethyst and a rare vaseline.

WILD FLOWER (NORTHWOOD)

The only place I've ever seen this pattern is on the outside of Northwood's Blossomtime compotes and that's a real shame. It is a beautiful pattern and certainly deserves better.

WILD LOGANBERRY (DEWBERRY)

Since I first showed this Westmoreland pattern in the pitcher and announced the existance of wines and goblets, other shapes have turned up including a covered compote, creamer, sugar and an open compote. All except the marigold wine have been iridized milk glass, but other colors may exist.

WILD ROSE

This well-known Northwood pattern is used on the exterior of two types of bowls. The first is an average flat bowl, often with no interior pattern. The second, however, is an unusual footed bowl, rather small, with an edge of open work in fan-like figures. Certainly, the intricacy of this open work took much care and skill. The colors are marigold, amethyst, green and occasionally pastels.

WILD ROSE LAMP

This very scarce lamp is found in three sizes and three colors, amethyst, green and marigold. The font is of clear glass but the remainder of the lamp is well-iridized. The Wild Rose pattern is well raised and meandering around the base of the lamp is a pattern of sunken dots. Occasionally one of these lamps is found with three medallions on the underside. These medallions contain portraits of three ladies believed to be wives of the three major stockholders of the Millersburg Company. One of these lamps would be a credit to any glass collection and certainly deserves top billing in a collection of Millersburg glass.

Wide Panelled Cherry

216

Wide Panel Epergne

Wide Rib Vase

Wild Blackberry

Wild Flower

Wildflower (Northwood)

Wild Loganberry Pitcher

Wild Rose

Wide Panel Vt.

Wild Rose Lamp

WILD ROSE SYRUP

Seen only in marigold of rich color and adequate lustering, the Wild Rose Syrup is very attractive. The maker is thus far unknown, but the mold work is quite similar to that of many of Harry Northwood's products. Measuring 6½″ tall, the Syrup holds 12 fluid ounces and has a metal top.

WILD ROSE WREATH (MINIATURE INTAGLIO)

The Butler Brothers ad showing this rare and desirable miniature call it a "stemmed almond" so we know it was intended as a nut cup and was made by U.S. Glass. It stands 2½″ tall and is usually about 3″ across the top. The design is intaglio and the only color reported is marigold.

WILD STRAWBERRY

One might think of this as the "grown-up" version of the regular Northwood Strawberry since it is much the same. The primary difference is the addition of the blossoms to the patterning and, of course, the size of the bowl itself, which is about 1½″ larger in diameter.

WINDFLOWER

Not one, but two shards of this pattern were excavated at the Dugan site, including a marigold bit and a sizeable chunk of an ice blue nappy with a portion of the handle attached. To the best of my knowledge, this pattern has not been reported previously in pastels. Windflower is an uncomplicated, well-balanced design with the background stippled and a geometric bordering device. The exterior is plain. Windflower is found on bowls, plates and handled nappies. The colors are marigold, cobalt, ice blue and ice green.

WINDMILL

Again, here is one of the best selling Imperial patterns, reproduced in the 1960s. It is still rather popular with collectors of old Carnival glass, especially in the darker colors. Originally, Windmill was made in a wide range of shapes, including berry sets, water sets, fruit bowls, pickle dishes, dresser trays and milk pitcher. The colors were marigold, green, purple, clambroth and smoke.

WINE AND ROSES

Please note the similarities between this scarce Fenton cider set, the well-known Lotus and Grape pattern shown elsewhere in this book, and the very rare water set called Frolicking Bears (maker unknown). Wine and Roses can be found in marigold in both pitcher and wine, and the wine is known in blue and the rare aqua.

WISHBONE

I personally feel that this Northwood pattern is one of the most graceful in Carnival glass. The lines just flow, covering much of the allowed space. Found on very scarce water sets, flat and footed bowls, plates and a very stately one-lily epergne, Wishbone is usually accompanied by the basketweave pattern on the exterior. My favorite color is the ice blue, but Wishbone is available in marigold, green, purple, blue, white and ice green. There is also a variant to this pattern.

Wild Rose Wreath
(Miniature Intaglio)

Wild Rose Syrup

Wild Strawberry

Windflower

Windmill

Wine and Roses

Wishbone

WISHBONE AND SPADES

I've always had misgivings about attributing this pattern, and I'm listing it here as a questionable Dugan one. As you can see, the design is a good one, well balanced and artistically sound. The shapes are berry sets and large and small plates and colors include peach opalescent, purple and green.

WISHBONE FLOWER ARRANGER

Similar in many ways to the Windsor Flower Arranger, for years I confused the two until one collector was kind enough to point out the differences. The Wishbone has an open top and none of the points touch while this isn't true with the Windsor.

WISTERIA

What a beautiful pattern this is! Certainly a first cousin to the Grape Arbor pattern in iridescent glass as well as the Lattice and Cherry pattern in crystal, Wisteria is unfortunately found only on water sets. While only tumblers in ice green have surfaced, both pitchers and tumblers are known in white and a really outstanding ice blue. What a shame no vivid colors are available in this Northwood masterpiece.

WOODEN SHOE

It seems as if good things come in bunches, and that's how it's been with miniatures in this book. However, one could never tire of seeing them and they are so rare, so here is another. The Wooden Shoe is 4½″ long and 3″ high. Its coloring is a light watery amber, and the glass is heavy.

WOODLANDS VASE

Once again I show a rare vase that is very impressive even though it measures only 5½″ tall. The coloring is a rich marigold with heavy lustre and the pattern is all smooth and raised. The design has a simple, well-balanced attractiveness that raises it above the everyday. And, of course, not many are known.

WOODPECKER VASE

The Woodpecker vase is 8¼″ long and measures 1⅝″ across the top. The only color I've run into is marigold, usually of good color. Perhaps this is strictly a Dugan pattern, and if so, it would explain the lack of other colors or shapes. These vases were usually hung in doorways or used as auto vases and were quite popular in their day.

WREATHED CHERRY

For many years, collectors have been puzzled by certain pieces of this pattern turning up with the Diamond Glass Company trademark, notably the covered butter. Now, since the Dugan shards have been catalogued, it becomes apparent this was a Dugan pattern. Known in berry sets consisting of oval bowls, table sets, water sets and a scarce toothpick holder, the colors are marigold, fiery amethyst, purple and white (often with gilt). The toothpick has been widely reproduced in cobalt, white and marigold, so beware! The only color in the old ones is amethyst.

WREATH OF ROSES (FENTON)

Known in bon-bons with or without stems, compotes, bowls and the punch set shown. Fenton's Wreath of Roses is a beautifully executed pattern. Two interior patterns are known. Colors are marigold, green, blue, amethyst, peach opalescent and white. The luster is very fine and the mold work excellent.

Wishbone Flower Arranger

Wishbone and Spades

Wisteria

Wooden Shoe

Woodlands Vase

Woodpecker Vase

Wreathed Cherry

Wreath of Roses

WREATH OF ROSES ROSEBOWL (DUGAN)

I've never understood while this little rosebowl has been grouped with the Fenton Wreath of Roses as one and the same pattern when it is obviously so different. So when a large hunk of Wreath of Roses Rosebowl was found among the Dugan shards, the explanation became obvious. They simply are not the same pattern! Found in marigold and amethyst, the Wreath of Roses Rosebowl has superior mold work and adequate finish.

WREATH OF ROSES VARIANT (DUGAN)

While Northwood, Fenton and Dugan all made similar patterns with this name, the Dugan is least known and valued. It hasn't all that much going for it since the design is weak and doesn't fill the space to advantage. Colors are amethyst, blue and marigold - at least the ones I've seen, but white, green and peach opal may exist.

ZIG-ZAG (FENTON)

I suspect the same mold shape was used for this nicely done Fenton water set and the Fluffy Peacock pattern. The Zig Zag was brought along in the enameled Carnival period and can be found in marigold, blue, green, amethyst, ice green and white. The floral work may vary slightly from piece to piece.

ZIG-ZAG (MILLERSBURG)

This lovely Millersburg bowl pattern is an improved version of a stippled ray theme but with a twist, resulting in a beautiful sun burst effect. This, coupled with a curious star and fan design on the exterior base, creates a unique and intriguing pattern. Colors are green, marigold and amethyst.

ZIPPERED HEART

Recent evidence that this is an Imperial pattern is a catalog from the company illustrating the Zippered Heart pattern in crystal in many shapes, including table sets, vases, compotes, rosebowls, a milk pitcher, punch sets and water sets. However, in iridized glass, the shapes I've seen are a berry set and the famous Queen's vase. While a beautiful purple is most encountered, marigold is known. Shown is a rare 5″ vase.

ZIPPER LOOP

While the Zipper Loop lamp is the most frequently encountered of all the kerosene lamps, it is a scarce item in itself. Known in four sizes, including a small hand lamp, the Zipper Loop is found in a good rich marigold color as well as a sparkling smoke finish. It has been reproduced in the former in the large size so be cautious when buying.

ZIPPER STITCH

This attractive piece shown is the tray for a lovely cordial set consisting of a decanter, six stemmed cordials and the tray. These were made in Czechoslovakia and are known only in marigold.

ZIPPER VARIANT

I suspect this nicely done covered sugar is of British origin, but can't be sure. The color is quite good as is the mold work. Note the interesting finial on the lid.

Wreath of Roses Variant (Dugan)

**Wreath
of Roses
Rosebowl**

Zig-Zag (Fenton)

**Zig-Zag
(Millersburg)**

Zippered Heart

Zipper Loop

Zipper Stitch

Zipper Variant

Schroeder's Antiques Price Guide

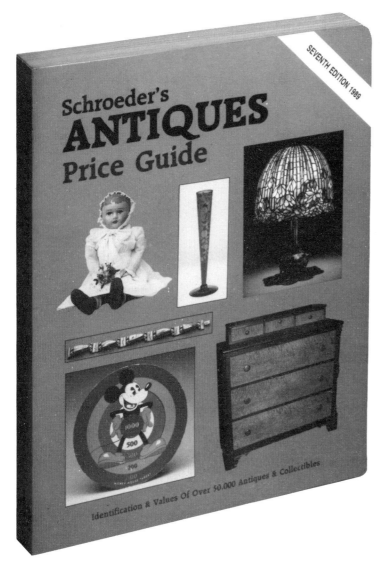

Schroeder's Antiques Price Guide has climbed its way to the top in a field already supplied with several well-established publications! The word is out, *Schroeder's Price Guide* is the best buy at any price. Over 500 categories are covered, with more than 50,000 listings. But it's not volume alone that makes Schroeder's the unique guide it is recognized to be. From ABC Plates to Zsolnay, if it merits the interest of today's collector, you'll find it in Schroeder's. Each subject is represented with histories and background information. In addition, hundreds of sharp original photos are used each year to illustrate not only the rare and the unusual, but the everyday "fun-type" collectibles as well -- not postage stamp pictures, but large close-up shots that show important details clearly.

Each edition is completely re-typeset from all new sources. We have not and will not simply change prices in each new edition. All new copy and all new illustrations make Schroeder's THE price guide on antiques and collectibles.

The writing and researching team behind this giant is proportionately large. It is backed by a staff of more than seventy of Collector Books' finest authors, as well as a board of advisors made up of well-known antique authorities and the country's top dealers, all specialists in their fields. Accuracy is their primary aim. Prices are gathered over the entire year previous to publication, from ads and personal contacts. Then each category is thoroughly checked to spot inconsistencies, listings that may not be entirely reflective of actual market dealings, and lines too vague to be of merit.

Only the best of the lot remains for publication. You'll find *Schroeder's Antiques Price Guide* the one to buy for factual information and quality.

No dealer, collector or investor can afford not to own this book. It is available from your favorite bookseller or antiques dealer at the low price of $12.95. If you are unable to find this price guide in your area, it's available from Collector Books, P. O. Box 3009, Paducah, KY 42001 at $12.95 plus $2.00 for postage and handling.

8½ x 11, 608 Pages $12.95

COLLECTOR BOOKS
A Division of Schroeder Publishing Co., Inc.